CHASING A DREAM
THE CARL ENGLISH STORY

CHASING A DREAM
THE CARL ENGLISH STORY

CARL ENGLISH WITH BLAKE MURPHY

FOREWORD BY STEVE NASH

FLANKER PRESS LIMITED
ST. JOHN'S

Library and Archives Canada Cataloguing in Publication

Title: Chasing a dream : the Carl English story / Carl English with Blake Murphy ; foreword by Steve Nash.
Names: English, Carl, 1981- author. | Murphy, Blake, 1986- author. | Nash, Steve, 1974- writer of foreword.
Description: Includes index.
Identifiers: Canadiana (print) 20190211113 | Canadiana (ebook) 20190211202 | ISBN 9781771177870 (softcover) | ISBN 9781771177887 (EPUB) | ISBN 9781771177894 (Kindle) | ISBN 9781771177900 (PDF)
Subjects: LCSH: English, Carl, 1981- | LCSH: Basketball players—Newfoundland and Labrador—Biography. | LCGFT: Autobiographies.
Classification: LCC GV884.E54 A3 2019 | DDC 796.323092—dc23

© 2019 by Carl English

PRINTED IN CANADA

This paper has been certified to meet the environmental and social standards of the Forest Stewardship Council® (FSC®) and comes from responsibly managed forests, and verified recycled sources.

Cover design by Mason Gulliver

FLANKER PRESS LTD.
PO BOX 2522, STATION C
ST. JOHN'S, NL
CANADA

TELEPHONE: (709) 739-4477 FAX: (709) 739-4420 TOLL-FREE: 1-866-739-4420
WWW.FLANKERPRESS.COM

9 8 7 6 5 4 3 2 1

We acknowledge the [financial] support of the Government of Canada. *Nous reconnaissons l'appui [financier] du gouvernement du Canada.* We acknowledge the support of the Canada Council for the Arts, which last year invested $153 million to bring the arts to Canadians throughout the country. *Nous remercions le Conseil des arts du Canada de son soutien. L'an dernier, le Conseil a investi 153 millions de dollars pour mettre de l'art dans la vie des Canadiennes et des Canadiens de tout le pays.* We acknowledge the financial support of the Government of Newfoundland and Labrador, Department of Tourism, Culture and Recreation for our publishing activities.

This book has been a long time coming, and writing it was a process that I was finally ready to face. I dedicate this book to my parents, Kevin and Lavinia English, and my uncle Junior McGrath. They are deeply missed but not forgotten and live strongly within me. Further dedications include my family, whom I enjoy and cherish every day: my beautiful wife, Mandy, and our three amazing children, Ryder, Kirsten, and Kylie; my brothers Peter, Brad, Kevin, and Michael; and Aunt Betty McGrath, Gerard, Howie, Chris, and Pamela McGrath. I'd also like to personally think anybody who helped me along during this amazing journey.

CONTENTS

Foreword

BY STEVE NASH

CARL ENGLISH HAS A STORY that won't disappoint. Newfoundland isn't known for its professional basketball players, but somehow this young fella who learned the game on a homemade hoop erected on the side of a two-lane highway would find his way to playing well over a decade of professional basketball in Europe and for his national team. I started to hear his name when he was playing for the University of Hawaii, and I always say if things had bounced a little differently, there's no doubt Carl would've had a good stint in the NBA.

Surviving a family tragedy can affect people in many ways. No matter the toll it took on Carl, he poured his heart into his game. His obsession grew, and out of it formed a legendary work ethic that dreams are made of. Watching his career, I was always drawn to the spark and confidence I could feel through the TV. A hot streak was always right around the corner, and his bravado was magnetic.

After years of only knowing Carl by phone or on TV, I got the chance to spend time with him and get to know him late in my career as general manager of the national team. It was apparent how important his wife and kids were to him. He always smiled when they came up, and it was obvious much of his motivation to play the game professionally for so long was to provide the best experience he could for them.

Having played all over top leagues in Spain and Greece, the stories are nearly as legendary as his work ethic. Beloved by his national team teammates for his sense of humour and quick tongue, everyone's got a "Carl story." Canada is known for its Newfie jokes, but with his cocky smile and joie de vivre, it seems like Carl always has the last laugh.

Michael English, Steve Nash, and Carl English at the Pan Am Games in Toronto, 2015, during which Canada won silver.

PROLOGUE

WE WEREN'T SUPPOSED TO BE THERE. If you look at my career—hell, my entire life—I *really* wasn't supposed to be there. So I took myself somewhere else.

It's March 10, 2001, in Tulsa, Oklahoma. I'm in my freshman year at Hawaii, and we're on an unlikely run as the No. 5 seed to the WAC Tournament final. We were up against Tulsa, and its home crowd makes for one of the most intense environments I've ever played in.

I've been seeing inconsistent minutes coming off of a redshirt year but have begun taking on more of a role down the stretch. It's been a struggle for me, mentally, trying to find my place and being so far from home. My minutes are low enough that most people still don't really know what I can do. But things are about to change.

We went down early but kept the game close and are down by two with a few seconds to play. I have 16 points off the bench. It may be my best game of the year already, and the season's about to come down to one possession, so I feel good. With an NCAA Tournament berth on the line, I think everyone thought Predraeg Savović, our top scorer and future NBA player, would get the ball. With the game I'm having, though, I know there's a chance I might.

There's a lot going on in a moment like that. Our whole season comes down to one shot. The crowd is crazy. It's easily the biggest game of my career to that point, and one of my best. It's tough to slow your mind down in these situations. There's so much that's led to this point—hard work, obstacles, and in my case, a lot of tragedy—and I have to battle to stay focused.

Before the final play, I close my eyes and take a deep breath. I'm not at the Reynolds Center. I'm not shooting on its rims. There aren't 8,160 people hoping I'll fail. I'm alone. It's just me, my basketball, and a homemade net along the side of Route 100 back in Patrick's Cove, Newfoundland. With the WAC final down to one possession, I take myself back there, back home, visualizing my next shot coming on my wood basket in front of Aunt Betty and Uncle Junior's place.

Our coach, Riley Wallace, draws the play up for Savović, but Tulsa defended it well. The ball finds its way to me. I attack the lane driving right, and when the help comes, I switch to my left hand to finish. With 1.8 seconds left on the clock, I rise and go off glass and in. It's the biggest shot of my life.

In overtime, I score seven more points to finish with 25, a game and season high. I go to the free-throw line four times in OT. I've had a bit of a rough season shooting free throws and an even worse start to the game at the line, so each time I try to settle my nerves by taking myself back home. In my mind, I shoot every one of those free throws on the side of the road, the Atlantic Ocean in the background. We finish the upset, beating Tulsa 78-72, and I'm named tournament MVP.

Not many people knew about me then. I was a redshirt freshman from a place in Canada nobody had heard of, on a mid-major with up-and-down playing time. They were about to learn, though. We'd just punched our ticket to the NCAA Tournament, which would bring March Madness to Newfoundland and my story to a national audience.

My life was about to change, and my career was about to take me down an incredible and improbable path. It all started with a Newfie kid and his homemade net on the side of the highway.

A basketball hoop Carl English made with his uncle Junior McGrath, on which Carl practised in Patrick's Cove, Newfoundland.

The gravesite of Carl English's parents, Kevin and Lavinia English, located in Branch, Newfoundland.

1

TRAGEDY. THE FIRE AND AFTERMATH.

MY PARENTS DIED WHEN I WAS FIVE. I don't remember much about the fire.

Family photo. Kevin and Lavinia English and their five sons, (L-R) Bradley, Kevin, Michael, Carl, and Peter.

I remember playing with new toys that morning. When you grow up in a small town in Newfoundland, "going into town" is a big deal. Every three or four months, my parents would take me and my four brothers on the two-hour drive from Branch, where we lived, to St. John's. It was always special for us, because we knew we'd get a couple of toys or snacks that you don't get at the stores in and around Branch. We went into St. John's that week, the Thursday before Easter weekend, and I was playing Cowboys and Indians with my new toys somewhere in the house on Good Friday morning.

That's when I heard my mom, Lavinia, screaming. My mom was screaming, and my dad was yelling. I remember smoke starting to fill the house and coming into the room we were playing in.

I only remember parts of the chaos and the details. A lot of what I know was told to me later by my brothers, family, and neighbours. I was only a kid at the time—my recollection of the day isn't all that great because I was so young and scared. One of my brothers is the same. People remember what they want to remember and try to block out what they need to block out.

Something went wrong when my dad, Kevin, was lighting the stove. At one point, I'd heard that he used boat fuel instead of the proper oil for the stove, but forensics didn't find any gas. My brothers remember my mom always going on about keeping the chimney clean, otherwise the house would burn down. What they told us later was that when Dad lit the fire, there was a sort of backdraft that blew back toward my parents. It blew fire around the kitchen, and my dad's shirt and some other things caught on fire. Mom went over to help Dad, and her nightdress caught on fire. The whole house was beginning to burn.

My brothers said everything happened quickly. Peter, my oldest brother, helped me get out. He ran downstairs to see what was going on but saw smoke everywhere and was having trouble breathing.

He came back upstairs, grabbed me and my younger brother Michael, and took us outside onto the roof of the cellar through a window. Our neighbour, Mr. Quigley, saw what was going on and came over and helped Peter get us down off the roof.

Bradley got out through a window on the second floor and jumped down to the ground. Kevin Jr., my older brother, had been downstairs and got out through the front door.

Somehow, all five of us brothers got out safely. We were all fine, hardly a scratch on us, but it was the scariest experience of our lives.

My parents weren't as lucky. They'd both been so close to the fire when it started and were so focused on stopping it and making sure we were okay that they were injured by the time they got out.

When we got outside, we all ran to get away from the house. When we turned back, there were flames and smoke everywhere. The house was in a blaze. We were helpless. My parents were rolling on the grass to try to put themselves out. Neighbours were coming from every-where, and there was screaming and shouting from every direction.

I was just a little kid. I was in complete shock. All I wanted was my mom. I was trying to look for her, and everyone had to keep me settled down and keep me from running back toward the house to her.

My mom was badly burned. She went to the neighbour's house across the street to lay in the bathtub to keep cool until the ambulance arrived. Being in rural Newfoundland in the 1980s, it took a while for ambulances and fire trucks to arrive. They took me in to see my mom while she lay in the tub. I was crying and scared, but at least I was with my mom.

My memory gets foggy after that, but I remember little things. I can remember the pyjamas that I was wearing. I can remember the boats on the wallpaper in our room as smoke started coming in. I can remember the toys I was playing with. I can remember the flames, and the panic, and how scared I was. And I remember sitting with my mom while she soaked in the tub, the last time I ever saw her.

Mom died at the hospital soon after arriving due to oxygen complications. Dad died from his injuries a few days later.

* * * * *

The thing about losing your parents so young is that you can't understand it. It hit me much harder later. When I was an adult, I found out the fire didn't kill my mother. The hospital made a mistake with one of her oxygen tubes. Maybe 20 years later, a nurse explained all of this to Peter. As he understood it, the family talked with lawyers at the time and decided not to do anything about it legally. This was incredibly difficult to learn. My brothers and I had to process my mother's death all over again with that new information.

You never truly heal from something like that, but as an adult, at least you can try to understand. As a child, they're just gone, and you can't comprehend why or what that means.

I didn't fully understand the impact until I had a family of my own. Now, when I leave for a week, my kids are lost. They're calling me every day, they're FaceTiming me, asking when I'm coming home. My five-year-old sleeps with a picture of me when I'm on the road. I was five when I lost my parents and my whole world went upside down, and it didn't really get put into context until I had my own kids. Now I can comprehend what that loss did to me over my life and what a piece of me was missing, because I see it in my own kids and understand that relationship between parents and children.

I remember some of the funeral. I was only five, so I didn't understand what was going on, but I remember being there and being very sad. I think I tried to do what my older brothers did and tried to stay close to them. It was overwhelming, at that age, all those eyes on me and my brothers, and I wasn't equipped to process it.

I remember everyone was so nice, and I remember not truly understand why. But that's small-town Newfoundland. Everyone always tries to pick each other up. Everyone has each other's backs. We lost everything we had when the house burned down, and I remember people coming by and giving us clothes. It's touching, looking back on it, but at the time, as a kid, it was confusing.

I've carried the loss of my parents my entire life. It's always been there. But so much about their loss hit me when I started figuring out who I was, when I began on my basketball path, and when I started my own family. At the time, it was sadness and confusion.

Family photo taken in Branch. Lavinia and Kevin English and their five sons, (L-R) Peter, Bradley, Kevin, Michael, and Carl.

* * * * *

5

The next few months were difficult for all of us, especially for me as one of the youngest.

The family had to figure out where the five of us would go, and nobody could take on all five of us, so right away our biggest support system, each other, was split up. At first we all lived with my aunt Florence for a couple of days while my parents' siblings figured out what was going to happen. That's how I ended up with Aunt Betty and Uncle Junior.

The family decided that Bradley would go to St. John's with Aunt Shirley. Kevin, Michael, and Peter would stay with Aunt Florence and Uncle David in Angels Cove. I would go with Aunt Betty. So, the five of us were split across three homes. Aunt Florence's was only about 10 minutes away, so three of my brothers weren't too far. The four of us would all be at the same school eventually, and we'd be able to see Bradley at Christmastime or in the summers. But we'd no longer live together. It wouldn't be like before. That's just the way it was.

The adjustment was hardest on me initially. The first week I stayed with Aunt Betty and Uncle Junior, I kept asking to go back and be with my older brothers. I cried at night and was eventually taken to Aunt Florence's in my pyjamas so I could see them. Then we'd try again the next day. Eventually, I got used to my brothers not being around.

Things got a bit easier as we got older. We began to accept our situation. It became what we knew. We were all together on Christmas and on some special occasions, and it was hard. I felt like I lost my parents and then my brothers were taken away from me. On top of this inexplicable tragedy, I had to adjust to a new family, all by myself.

The transition wasn't easy, even in a good home, which I'm thankful Aunt Betty and Uncle Junior provided me with. Aunt Betty was my mom's sister, and they were raised together in a foster family with

Aunt Florence's parents. Aunt Betty and Uncle Junior have four kids of their own, so it was hard at first to find my place in the family. Aunt Betty used to joke when she'd get interviewed later in my career: "When you got four kids, one more is not gonna matter a big difference." I became their baby at the time.

But it took some getting used to. Being the youngest and thrown into a new house, I had to discover the pecking order and my place within the family. I was already dealing with a lot, separated from my brothers, and I was always missing them, or my mom and dad. Every day seemed to get a little more difficult. I was trying to adjust to my cousins, to my aunt and uncle, who were doing everything they could for me, but who weren't, in the end, my mom and dad.

There were many nights that I found it got to me. As I got older, it started to hit me a bit more that my parents were dead, and I started questioning a lot of things. Were they proud of me? What were they really like—not just what people told me they were like? Was I more like my mom or my dad? What would life be like if they were still here? What would our family be like? There were so many questions.

There were a lot of long nights, the realization that my parents were dead, and the questions that accompanied their loss. It would always come up if it had been a hard day at school or a hard day with basketball or I'd gotten in trouble. Those tougher moments would trigger the sadness and loneliness. I started asking, "Why me?" In my darkest moments, I asked, "Why not me instead?" I cried myself to sleep, wondering. It comes up in everything that you go through, and it's the most personal thing, because those thoughts come right at you.

As a young boy, especially back then, I never talked about my feelings. It was always tough love. No one told me to express myself or asked how I was feeling, so I bottled everything up. I've always referred to it as the "hockey mentality." That's what people expect in that culture—a strong Newfoundlander. Even as I got older, being interviewed about the loss of my parents was never easy. It's still hard, today, to write about it.

I had a family supporting me, but I didn't communicate what I was going through. The people who could relate, my brothers, were at Aunt Florence's and Aunt Shirley's. When I got down, I couldn't ask if they were going through the same thing. I had a strong relationship with my brothers, especially Kevin and Michael because of basketball, but the freedom I felt from that was because of the basketball, not because we talked about things. I felt incredibly alone.

Looking back, going through it all alone developed in me some sort of drive, some sort of toughness. If I can get through this, I thought, nothing can stop me. Every day I woke up and had no choice but to find a way through the fog. I spent a lot of time dealing with what I was feeling inside and trying not to let it affect what I was doing outside. I learned to compartmentalize. And then as life went on and other things happened to me, I was a little more centred because, you know, what could happen to me that's any worse than what's already happened? I didn't get that until later, though. As a kid it was just frustrating and lonely and sad.

My aunt and uncle, though, were extremely understanding, and I'm grateful for their love and support. They knew when I was sad, when I was lonely, and they kept me connected to my parents. They took me on drives at night, we looked at the stars, and they told me the brightest ones were following me, shining down, and those were my parents.

That stuck with me, to always look for signs that they were still around. Some of the only things that made it out of the fire were pictures, and I still have them. The edges are burnt, but the pictures remain. They're something. Enough to help keep my parents' memory alive, to remember that Mom was beautiful and that Dad was always working for the family. In my twenties, I had both their faces tattooed on my back. Little things. A connection. So that they were always a part of my life.

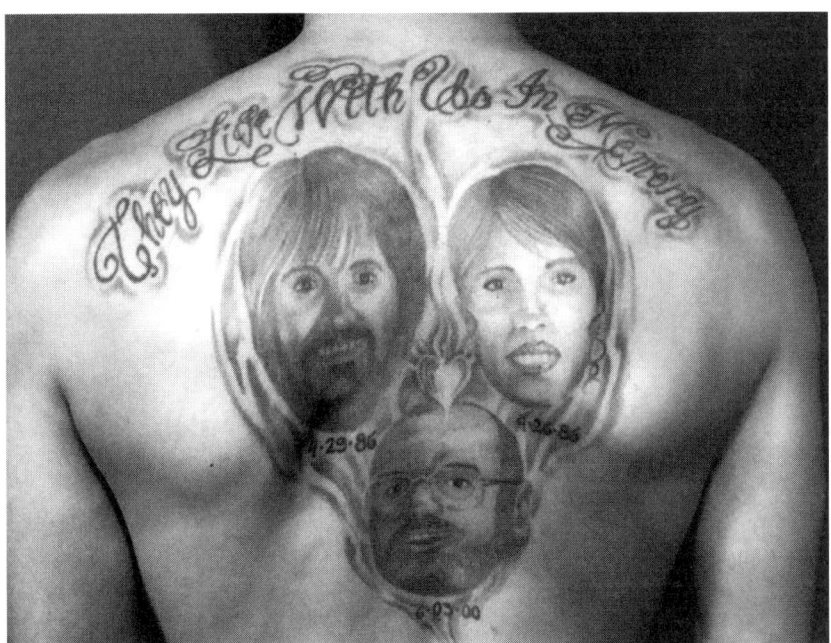

Carl English's memorial tattoo, which he had inked on his back in Gran Canaria, Spain: "They live with us in memory." The tattoo shows Carl's parents, Kevin and Lavinia, and his uncle Junior McGrath, and the dates of their deaths.

Whenever things were difficult later in life or on the basketball court, I reminded myself: My fan club is upstairs.

2

The Hoop. Childhood and Finding Basketball.

L IFE AT AUNT BETTY AND UNCLE JUNIOR'S eventually became my new normal. I got used to my aunt and uncle, and to living with my cousins instead of my brothers. As I got older, I had enough on my plate, with school and chores and sports, to keep myself moving, even if I was still sad and lonely sometimes.

It was my relationship with Uncle Junior that helped me push through. My uncle, Ignatious "Junior" McGrath, and I became close almost immediately.

He was 36 at the time I moved in. A few years earlier, he had suffered a stroke because of a fairly rare heart condition called arrhythmogenic right ventricular cardiomyopathy (AVRC), which left him without full function of the left side of his body. His left hand and left foot, in particular, were limited. But that didn't slow him down. The way it works in rural Newfoundland is that if something is wrong with the car or truck, you fixed it. If the roof had a leak, you fixed it. You don't call a roofer or a mechanic unless maybe your neighbour happens to be a roofer or a mechanic. So Uncle Junior was a jack-of-all-trades handyman, but his left hand didn't work so well.

That's where I came in. By trade, Uncle Junior was a fisher person, and while my older cousins, Gerard, Howie, Chris, and Pamela, all helped out, as was expected of them, I was too young. So I became Uncle Junior's left-hand man when he wasn't on the family boat. Our entire relationship was built and balanced on us doing things together as a team. We did everything together and grew very close as a result.

Life in small-town Newfoundland was simple—we lived off the land and what the water provided. Anything we were able to manage on our own went a long way. My diet consisted mostly of fish and moose, we hunted rabbit and ducks, and we grew our own carrots and potatoes. Years later, as a pro athlete constantly being told to be mindful of my diet, I looked back on those years and laughed—I definitely ate organic in my youth, but I didn't have much choice in the matter.

Uncle Junior taught me to how to fish for trout, how to track for game, and how to snare rabbits. Since I couldn't help with the catch, I bagged and roped the nets and cut wood. We were dependent on the fishery, and as my cousins began moving out, my responsibilities increased. Eventually, I found myself on Uncle Junior's boat.

My cousins Gerard and Pam had gone away to school, Howie was working as a carpenter, and Chris was a welder, so I was the last one around to help. The three boys eventually all moved to Ontario for work, which was pretty standard back then. People either went to get their education or went away to work. My dad used to fish during the summer and then go to Alberta to work during the winter. He spent years doing that, because sometimes he didn't make enough fishing. If you ever listen to Newfoundland music, you'll hear all sorts of lyrics about heading to Ontario or Alberta. It was the way of life, and that was the path I figured I'd follow, too. For now, their path meant more responsibility for me.

Life on the boat was about more than fishing. We couldn't fish in the winter, but that didn't mean we had winters off. We spent the cold months preparing gear and getting ready for next season—we mended nets, prepared lobster pots, fixed up the boat. It was similar to sports, in a way. We had work to do in the off-season so that when spring came around, everything, including us, was ready.

The work came naturally to me—these were normal chores for a Newfoundland boy. My wife, Mandy, who was my girlfriend at the time, bagged nets with her father when she was growing up in nearby St. Bride's. But I wasn't much help with the catch. Life on the boat wasn't for me—my family likes to remind folks about my bouts with seasickness. But I didn't have a choice. The work had to get done, and Uncle Junior couldn't do it himself.

In the process, we became nearly inseparable. Uncle Junior taught me about life, and I worked as his hands. We became as close as a father and son. I missed my parents, but life delivered a best friend in the form of my uncle as I coped with my loss.

When I found basketball, Uncle Junior became my biggest fan.

＊ ＊ ＊ ＊ ＊

I was seven when I first realized I really liked basketball.

At that time and in that part of Newfoundland, every kid played every sport. It wasn't nearly as organized or as structured as it is now or as in bigger cities. We had our gym classes, played sports during recesses, and then might have played whatever sport was in season after school. That meant baseball and softball in the summer and pond hockey and road hockey in the winter. It wasn't organized compared to the way it is with my kids now. We'd all just get together and go play. I ran cross-country and played volleyball in school for years, too.

I got to a certain age where most kids picked one sport because there's so much time and money involved. It wasn't like today, where parents make their kids specialize early to get an advantage. For us, everyone played everything, and then once it got expensive or took up a lot of time, there was only room for one.

Basketball was an easy choice for me. It was simple. I was good at it. The better I got, the more I loved it. Basketball became an obsession.

Gord Pike deserves a lot of credit for fuelling my basketball obsession. He was the gym teacher and basketball coach at Fatima Academy, which I attended from kindergarten to grade eleven. It was a small school—about 250 kids total across thirteen grades and five or six towns—so the teachers did a little bit of everything, including supervise students who were waiting for the school bus. I remember being in grades two and three and shooting with Gord while I waited for my ride home. It was only ten minutes or so here and there, shooting and playing Around the World, but it was a formative experience—I tasted basketball, and I wanted more. It was Gord who eventually gave me what would be the first of many versions of my homemade net along the side of the highway.

He gave me my first basketball rim, and Uncle Junior and I set to work trying to make a hoop. Over the years I'd make use of all kinds of different rims. At one point we had a bicycle wheel with the spokes beaten out of it attached to the shed. At another, I'd taken down our town's only stop sign to use as a backboard. Another time, my cousin Chris welded a rim for me. That rim was so thick that if my shot caught too much rim I'd be chasing the ball, so I learned to shoot for swishes pretty early. Those rims probably helped, because soft rims are too friendly. So, getting a real rim was a big deal.

At first we tried it out in the yard, but there was no pavement back there. I'd be dribbling on rocks and grass and sometimes snow, and that's pretty hard, although it probably improved my handle in the long run. The ground was rough, and we couldn't just pay to pave it over, and there were no outdoor courts in our community. Baseball and hockey and volleyball were all a little easier to come up with makeshift places to play, but there was nothing for basketball.

One day I got it in my head to pave the yard myself. I went around and picked up little bits of asphalt that used to come off the roads during the winter. I went and got the wheelbarrow, and I'd wheel it around and pick up all of these chunks of pavement. Once I had enough, a neighbour helped me put it in a drum and light the drum on fire to melt the pavement down. Once it was melted, we poured it all over the dirt. It was only enough for a seven-by-eight-foot patch. It wasn't much better than the gravel, but to me it was worth trying.

Everyone around town used to think I was crazy for doing stuff like this. That wasn't even the half of it yet. By the time I was eight or nine, I'd gotten another rim for Christmas from Santa and had started to get a pretty good jumpshot. Now I wanted to try dunking, too. So, one version of the net was built out from the back a little bit so that I could try to jump off of a rock and dunk. I'd be out there for hours playing until I got called in for bed or it got too dark to see the rim.

Even with the homemade pavement, there were plenty of issues. My net would always blow over on windy days, and I decided I needed a sturdier rig. So, Uncle Junior and I would go down to get some sticks cut at the sawmill, which was the cheapest way to build one, and I'd go about trying my next monstrosity. On maybe my tenth construction, I built the one that never came down. Wind could rattle it but couldn't blow it over, and even though it didn't look like much, all I needed was for it to stay standing.

Carl English as a boy in Patrick's Cove, Newfoundland, practising basketball on homemade pavement in his yard.

There was still a problem. The pavement we'd made wasn't as good as when I'd dribble along the road, and that would give me more space and a better surface. I pleaded with Aunt Betty for what felt like years to let me move the net to the road.

Route 100 is just one lane in each direction cutting through the Cape Shore. The traffic is pretty light. Most times it was people passing by to go to somewhere else, usually the Cape St. Mary's Ecological Reserve, where tourists would always go birdwatching. As kids, we'd always look for licence plates from different provinces or countries, because it was almost always tourists. Occasionally, trucks would come through, too. My argument was that it was open enough that I'd be able to see cars coming well ahead of time to stay safe.

Eventually, Aunt Betty relented and let me move it to the road. I got my way, and it just made me more committed to playing all the time. I'd have to keep tweaking the net as new issues came up. Once we moved it onto the road, I was shooting up against a thirty-foot drop, so if I missed, I was chasing the ball down a meadow, and on the other side there was a dike full of water. So, that meant I needed green fishing net, which was also our volleyball net, along the back to catch the ball. There was also a fish tub with rocks to weigh it down and keep it from falling, and the four-by-four posts were reinforced with bits of stop signs and whatever else I could find. Each change was a little better than the last, so I never minded putting in the work.

We only had one close call with the net on the road. There was one beautiful summer day when we heard a bang from indoors. A tractor-trailer had been out in St. Bride's to pick up the fish and was driving through. I had left my rim up the night before instead of taking it down. When I'd first put the net out there, I kept rolling my ankle when I landed, so I'd altered the net so the rim stuck out a little bit more and I had more flat ground to land on. It normally wasn't an issue, because by that time the whole town knew my routine and that I'd be playing there.

Well, the tractor-trailer caught the rim sticking out and knocked the net over. Aunt Betty was worried we were going to be in trouble for damaging the truck. Meanwhile, I was storming around the house, mad at the truck driver for knocking my net over.

Once we moved the net, I was shooting on this monster rig with the Atlantic Ocean in the background. Depending on the day, there was a backdrop of blues and greens or greys, and I could hear the ocean as I was playing. It was just fresh air and quiet. I might not hear anything other than some birds chirping and dog's barking, and then the ocean. I was used to living in Newfoundland, but those sounds and that feeling close to the water were always special. The weather isn't always the friendliest, though. Usually, if it was miserable one day, you'd know it would be nice the next, but it didn't bother me much either way.

I'd be out there shooting with frost on the rims if I needed to. Part of the winter routine was shovelling the snow off the road to clear a space to play. Other kids would come out and join, too. They'd just get off the bus at our place after school and stay and play, or my brothers Kevin and Michael would come play one-on-one to seven in trios. We'd all be out there with mittens on in the winter. They'd leave bored or cold and I'd be out there another couple of hours. One of our neighbours, John McGrath, used to joke about hearing the ball bouncing at seven in the morning or ten at night and saying some choice words, but he and all the other neighbours were supportive.

I think everyone knew eventually that it wasn't just a phase for me.

* * * * *

By the time I was in grade six, I was playing on the junior team at Fatima, which was usually for grades seven to nine. Because the school covered every grade, if you were good enough, you were able to go play with the older kids.

I was the youngest kid on the team, and every opponent made sure I knew it. Coach Pike put me in a game for the first time, and my first two plays were disasters. On the first, I couldn't get the ball over half-court. On the second, I was going so fast I couldn't stop, and I ended up sliding into the wall and getting called for a travel. Everyone was poking fun at me, but I couldn't stop with the sneakers I was wearing.

I blamed the shoes. I had these X-Calibers. It sounds funny now, but they were ASICS, and they were a popular shoe. Complex called them one of the eighty greatest sneakers of the 1980s. At that time, if I wanted new shoes, I had to save up to buy them. I did all sorts of odd jobs to get a few dollars together here and there. We always had to help with the catch and our chores around the house, but we got to keep anything we made doing our own jobs.

We could always make ends meet at Aunt Betty and Uncle Junior's—we just didn't have the extras. They did everything possible to make sure we had food on the table and clothes on our backs and the environment we needed to be successful. Those times in Newfoundland, feeding a family of five on a fishing business could be difficult. When I first moved in, three of us boys shared one room, my two cousins in a bunk bed and me on a cot. It's just the way things were. If the price of cod was down or we didn't catch our quota that season, it was tough. That was for the majority of families and communities, not just ours, and everyone understood that.

I'd go around and pick up bottles in ditches and cash those in. I'd pick bakeapples in town. It was a lot of picking to get a bucketful of those, but I'd get pretty good money for those. The most lucrative job was cutting out cod tongues. The tongue of the codfish is considered a delicacy, and you could sell them to tourists for four or five dollars per dozen. When I was a little older, I'd go down to St. Bride's to the hopper, which was where the fish plant would throw out all the fish heads. I'd go through all the fish heads and cut out all the tongues, and I'd have this big gallon bucket of tongues that was worth $50 or $80, depending on the haul and the season.

Carl English's basketball team playing in the 3A provincials final game. Taken at Fatima Academy in St. Bride's, Newfoundland, where Carl went to school.

I was taught a valuable lesson early on: I had to work for the finer things. And when I got them, I had to take care of them. With the money I made, I always had eyes on a new pair of shoes. When I got a new pair, they'd have to last me at least a year. It would take a lot of work to save up for a $150 pair of Pippens or Jordans, so I'd clean those things with a toothbrush to make sure they lasted.

It was the same kind of lesson with chores. When I got home from school, I might get away with a little bit of basketball, but before long I was getting called to cut wood or do my homework. I remember Aunt Betty yelling down to the road, "Stop bouncing that ball! Get your books!" I had to get my work done first before I could get back to shooting.

My aunt was fairly strict, because she had to be. She had four boys and a girl, and she wanted us to do as best as we could, so she ran a tight roster. I think my brothers and cousins affected that, too. Her second-oldest, Howie, and my oldest brother, Peter, were in the same class and were pretty wild. I think she wanted to make sure I wouldn't be too wild and crazy and have that same partying streak. If you get in trouble in a small town, it kind of gets escalated and everyone knows, so she wanted to keep me on the straight and narrow.

I didn't understand it at the time, but it was all worth it. Growing up here in these small towns, people either got in trouble or played sports. I managed to stay out of trouble, mostly. I never drank or anything like that. I still don't, actually. I'll have a glass of wine or one of those fruit drinks like a Palm Bay and the boys will all laugh at me, but I've never been drunk. Since I was a kid, I was goal-oriented, and basketball meant so much to me that those vices weren't a temptation.

A lot of the time, Uncle Junior would sit up in the window watch me play all day. He'd tease me a lot about it. Once I was playing more competitively, he'd harass me if I didn't play well. As I got more committed to it, he did, too, and he'd always be the one driving me to games or tournaments. That was another big part of what made us grow so close. He was my biggest supporter.

The rest of the family did their best to support, too. At that time, we only had two channels: CBC and NTV. We didn't get any NBA games when I was growing up. There were hardly ever any sports other than the hockey game. Steve Nash didn't get big enough to be on our channels until the late 1990s, maybe even later. When my oldest cousin, Gerard, went away to college, he used to tape NBA games, so I was able to watch those.

Over and over, I'd watch a tape of Michael Jordan playing against the Pistons with Marv Albert on the call. I'd try to replicate every move Jordan made. As I got older, my brothers and cousins would tape more games for me and bring the tapes back from Ontario, so I'd get to watch other players and try to replicate guys like Nash. I'd see something and try it over and over until I could do it, too. It makes me wonder what I could have done with the access to YouTube that players have today, because I was relentless. I'd get a new ball for my birthday, and two months later you could see the tread because I'd played every day. A new ball was like a piece of gold to me. I always wanted to be out there playing.

Basketball was my escape, my way out. Whenever I felt lonely and missed my brothers, or was sad about my parents, basketball lifted the clouds. Basketball made me feel free. School troubles, issues on the playground, everything went away when I was playing ball. And the conditions didn't matter. If it was windy, I'd work on my handle. If it was clear, it was a shooting day. The game became my passion and instilled in me a work ethic I didn't know I had. Basketball helped me cope. And that's why I loved it.

And I was damn good at it. So good that I started thinking it was a way out, in more ways than one.

3

PASSION. BASKETBALL IN NEWFOUNDLAND.

I RECOVERED JUST FINE from my first taste of playing with the juniors in grade six. If I was committed before, I was obsessed now. I played on my net every day, as much as I could, seven or eight hours most days. I wasn't going to be laughed at again.

Grade eight junior boys' team. Teammates in front row are Brian Careen, Michael English, Carl English, and George English. Coach Melvin Critch at right with Kevin English.

I made the junior team for grades seven, eight, and nine again when I was in grade seven. I'd improved so much—and grown enough—that they put me on the senior team, too. I was playing junior with kids up to two years older than me and senior with kids up to five years older. The senior level was a tough adjustment because of the size and physicality, and between that and dominating the junior level, it was great for my game. I kept getting better, and each of those challenges pushed me harder.

By the time I was in grade eight, I was a lot better at the senior level. I wasn't a force, being so much younger, but I was holding my own and playing consistently. I still played junior, too, putting up some ridiculous numbers, even up to provincials there. I won most valuable player for the junior team. That started to get me noticed around the province, because it looked like I could dominate come high school.

Grade eight was also the first year I had a chance to play on a bigger stage. I tried out for the Newfoundland fifteen-and-under team, which I was pretty sure I was good enough to make. That team was led by the coach from St. Francis High School in Harbour Grace, and he ended up picking three of the kids from his own team for that provincial team, while I was one of the last cuts. I was devastated, but we'd meet up again.

These little things stuck with me. I felt like I should have made it. I made a little mental note, because Newfoundland is small enough that you know you're going to see these players and coaches again. Just like after grade six, I was possessed that summer. All I cared about was getting better and proving them wrong for cutting me from that team.

That was always the thing with me. A pattern was developing in my life. The bumps in the road always made me work harder, dig deeper, in order to overcome them. Whatever was holding me back could be overcome so long as I put in the work.

We played against St. Francis in one of the first tournaments in grade nine, and all three of the players the coach had picked over me were on that team. My coach, Coach Pike, came up to me before the game and whispered: "You remember what they did to you last year, right?" I don't remember the exact total, but I must have put up sixty or seventy points in that game. Grade nine was going to be my big breakout season at the senior level, and that set the stage.

By that point I was dominating junior. I'd play five minutes on, five minutes off, and still put up big numbers. The senior team was my focus, and that year we won provincials for 1A schools. At Fatima, we came from around the bay, so the school was small enough that our team was mostly made up of whoever wanted to play. Meanwhile, we were going up against townie teams, which was what we called teams from St. John's, who had maybe 1,500 kids to choose from in our age groups. We'd been so close the year before and were now just heads above the other 1A teams, winning a lot of games by twenty points or more, so we were going to be bumped to 2A for the following season.

I made the Newfoundland team the summer after grade nine, which was my first taste of representing my province or my country. The tournament was in Prince Edward Island, so I got to travel, which was a really cool experience at fifteen. At that point I was still a scrawny kid. I was five foot ten, maybe five foot eleven, but the coaches kept me at point guard, which was where I was best off playing and was probably best for my development, too. I got an all-star award at that tournament, which I felt showed I should have made the team the summer before and that I was one of the best players in the province.

We came in fourth or fifth, which was really good for Newfoundland, but despite the success, I left with a bad taste in my mouth. The coach of that team wasn't happy with me after the tournament. He made me cry in the locker room after our final game. I was an all-star, and he basically told me I'd never play on another Newfoundland team again if I didn't change who I was as a player. It really hurt at the time, but it served as more motivation to keep working. It lit a fire inside of me.

⋆ ⋆ ⋆ ⋆ ⋆

The bumps in the road always made me work harder to overcome them.

I told myself that, because I played basketball so much, I could play until I mastered what was holding me back. Whenever I set my mind on reaching a goal, I worked hard to make sure it became a reality. I didn't have anyone cracking the whip, telling me to pick up a cone and dribble a ball and put down a cone, or whatever the drills are now. Looking back at it now, some of it seems silly, but I did whatever it took. I didn't know better. We didn't have access to the Internet or Instagram or anything like that. Everything I did had to be self-taught.

I had the love and passion, and I had a ball. I didn't care which kind. I made a surface, or I didn't need one. I'd dribble on rocks or grass. I'd dribble on my bed because I thought it would make my forearms stronger. I would tie my right arm behind my back to force myself to work on my left. I'd do wall sits half the night and calf raises on the bathtub. I would run sprints on the hills. Anything I thought would make me better.

One of my brothers brought me a basketball magazine from Ontario, and there was an ad for Jumpsoles, these big platforms you could strap to your shoes to help improve your vertical jump. They were about $200, so they were out of the question for me. But I had to have them. I cut up a bunch of pairs of old shoes and nailed and glued them together. Then I put them on top of my shoes and taped the whole rig together, and I would run up and down the road. I wonder why I have bad ankles now. Well, back then I was just thinking of anything that could make me better. I did the dumbest stuff. I was just infatuated with being good.

I wasn't playing against great competition, but I was playing more than anybody else. My whole high school career, we practised one day a week, on Thursday evening. Then we'd play for fifteen minutes at recess and forty-five minutes at lunch every day. For most kids, that was it. For me, I'd play every evening once I got off the bus until it got dark around five thirty, and all day on the weekends once my chores were done.

I was really lucky with all the support I had around me that allowed me to commit to basketball. Aunt Betty and Uncle Junior and my brothers were always very supportive. Some of Uncle Junior's family were our neighbours, too, and they were the same way. My wife, Mandy's, family was great, too. I've known Mandy and her family for my entire life, really. Her mom and dad were amazing and did everything to help me, and Mandy was and always has been incredible.

Once our teams became good, everyone in the community loved basketball. These small towns were always supportive, and when we were winning, they took it to another level. If we won a tournament, there would be a motorcade of cars waiting for our bus on the way home. We'd be hanging out the windows, banging on the bus, as dozens of cars followed us through the towns, honking to let everyone know we won. That was always fun, and I really looked forward to it on the way home.

Coach Pike has been an influence and mentor for me my whole life. He became a father figure for me coming up in school, being my coach and always looking out for me. He'd be there for rides home from school, after practice or after games, whether it was cross-country or basketball. In Newfoundland at that time, we'd hitchhike if we didn't have a ride. We would just go out on the road toward home with a thumb out, and someone would eventually give us a lift. There wasn't a lot of traffic, so teachers would often be the ones driving us home.

Coach Pike and I would ride together to and from games or tournaments, or when I needed a lift home, and we'd have these chats. He was always motivating me, right up through high school. To this day we're still close, and I'll turn to him if I need advice. He was the first one who believed in me and helped me develop my passion for basketball. It was important for me to have that kind of an influence in my life.

Basketball was so important to me that it helped determine who I was becoming. Using it as an escape helped develop my drive. The way my family and the community around me showed support built my values. I was always good in school, but I found that I learned more from playing basketball and my teammates and my coaches than I ever could in a classroom.

* * * * *

The senior season when I was in grade ten was a lot of fun. My brother Kevin was on that team, and so was my neighbour Desi, who would always come over to my place after school to practise and play with me.

Coach Pike always put Kevin and me together when we travelled for tournaments. We would be billeted out on the road and stay at another family's house. He always made sure Kevin and I were together, and with the younger team he would make sure Michael and I were together. I loved that. I looked forward to that part of the trips as much as the basketball itself. Other friends on the team would ask to room together, but I'd always want to stay with my brothers, because I didn't get to live with them. That played a big part in our being able to build a special bond even though we were separated from each other. It was crucial to me at that stage in my life.

We were even more dominant and got bumped a division again. It was great to be able to share in that success with my brother.

The summer after grade ten, the coach who hurt me with his remarks when I was on the fifteen-and-under team was coaching the seventeen-and-under team, so I refused to play. Instead, I tried out for the nineteen-and-under team that would be representing Newfoundland at the Canada Summer Games in Brandon, Manitoba. I made that team at just sixteen and was one of the youngest people competing in the games. Kevin should have made that team, too. He got cut, but we still got to go to Manitoba together because he wound up making the team for track.

This was also one of the first events I attended where there was some media coverage, so there were clips on the news of me playing in a jersey with Dunkaroos as the sponsor, and the coach calling me the best athlete on the team. That was a lot of fun to experience for the first time.

I almost didn't get to go. The coaches, Glen Normore, Clarence Sutton, and George Power, who are all legends in Newfoundland basketball, really pushed for me to make the team. Because I was only sixteen, they had to get approval from my aunt to let me play.

Once she said yes, we had to fundraise so I could pay to go. This was where the spirit of community in Newfoundland always showed itself, and it started to make me into a better person. The whole community would get behind us. Not just me and my brothers, either, but anyone who would make these teams. It would be a full community effort, from card games and bingo games to raffles, anything at all the towns could do to raise enough so we could make the most of these opportunities. All of these things were very important in my upbringing.

There are a lot of good things about small-town Newfoundland. That security and support are huge. You hear people say it takes a village to raise a child, and that's true about Newfoundland. There were many, many people involved in my development from a young kid right on through.

The Canada Games were a cool experience. By the end of the tournament, I was playing a lot more and even started some games. I was such a basketball geek that the age difference didn't matter. I would watch guys and study their games, trying to find ways to adapt my game to fit in. If other guys were out partying or socializing, I was focusing on basketball. Getting to play up a few age levels and against even better competition was good for my development.

That same level of competition wasn't there back in Newfoundland for grade eleven. We were pretty dominant that year, even up another division, and at that point I was a six-foot-three or six-foot-four point guard. That was around when I dunked for the first time.

We only lost three times that whole season, and all three losses were to St. Francis in Harbour Grace. It was the same coach who had cut me, and they still had the same three guys he had chosen over me.

As fate would have it, we were matched up with them in the championship game. Our gym at Fatima wasn't very big, but the towns packed it. Fans were lined up all the way to the court line just to fit everyone in. It was the most people I'd ever seen at a game. It still gives me goosebumps to think about. Kevin brought one of those police megaphones and was getting the crowd going. Other people had fog-horns. The place was rocking.

There was no way I was losing this game. Not with what I felt they had done to me, and not with my third straight provincial title in the balance. They didn't want it more than I did.

When the game ended, I climbed a ladder underneath our home basket and cut down the final piece of the net. I draped it around my neck and played to the crowd. We had won the championship. I had come full circle from my first basketball disappointment. I had proven everything I had set out to—to the provincial coach, to St. Francis, and to myself.

It was to be the last high school game I played in Newfoundland.

* * * * *

Fatima Academy beat St. Francis High School in the final game of the 3A provincials in 1998, when Carl English was in grade eleven. It was the last game Carl played in Newfoundland. Pictured is Carl cutting down the net after the game.

By the end of grade eleven in 1998, a pair of brothers from Mount Pearl, Tim and Steve Beckett, had become the first Newfoundlanders to play Division I basketball. For the first time, the idea of using basketball to earn a scholarship seemed realistic. I was even more focused on improving, and I was looking for ways to get better.

There was a local men's division where some university players would play, and the games were high-quality. I'd go and play really well against these grown men. One time we put in our Canada Games team and held our own at that level, which was great for a bunch of teenagers. One of the Beckett brothers came to check out one of those games, and I struggled in the first half and then went off in the second.

I was starting to think bigger. But it was a different time, when I was coming up, one today's average basketball fan will find hard to comprehend. The Internet makes everything easier. Teams can scout players from far away—players can put their highlight tapes on You-Tube or Instagram. It's easier to get noticed and get better now. If I

were coming up in this era, with the stuff I was doing in high school and with the provincial teams, I could have gone to any school I wanted without leaving home. I'd won three straight provincial titles, earned my team's MVP award, been named All-Canadian first team, and I was an honour roll student, but I kept being told my dreams weren't realistic.

Carl English practising on his homemade hoop in Patrick's Cove, Newfoundland, late 1990s.

People kept telling me I couldn't. They teased me and gave me a hard time about the idea of getting out of Newfoundland. I paid no attention. It wasn't about leaving just to leave. I'm a proud Newfoundlander. I wasn't even at the point yet where I was thinking I would be good enough to make the NBA.

I was sure I was good enough to get an education out of the game and keep playing it. But I needed to get noticed. Newfoundland, my home, became a bump in the road.

4

Risk. Leaving for Toronto.

"**I**'M MOVING AWAY."

I broke the news to Aunt Betty at the end of grade eleven.

"I want to get a scholarship," I told her. "I want to go to university, and I want to do whatever I can with basketball."

It was like trying to get her to let me move the net down to the road all over again. I just kept on her every day.

"You're crazy," she said. "How's it going to work?"

I knew what she was doing. She was trying to protect me. I was the youngest, the last one to go. I was a part of Aunt Betty's family. It's a big adjustment from Patrick's Cove to life in bigger cities. Once I was gone, that was it, I was gone.

At that point I had my heart set on St. Thomas Aquinas in Oakville, Ontario. I knew from my research that Ontario was where I should be going. The school had recently graduated a prospect to the National Collegiate Athletic Association (NCAA). I figured the school was on someone's radar and a place to get noticed in the United States.

I'd considered Eastern Commerce Collegiate, too, which was a powerhouse for a lot of that era. Jamaal Magloire had just come through there and was at Kentucky. My aunt thought it was in too

33

rough a neighbourhood, so she wasn't going to let me go there. The nice thing about St. Thomas Aquinas was that my cousin Howie and his wife, Lori, lived in Mississauga, twenty minutes west of Toronto. If I lived with him, I'd be right inside the zone to play there.

It's funny, looking back. I could have just gone to Father Michael Goetz Secondary School, where Andrew Nicholson played. It was just two minutes away, and it was the nearest hoop if I wanted to go play on my own once I moved. But they weren't in the magazines or the newsletters I had seen, and they hadn't sent anyone to the NCAA at that point. It wasn't St. Thomas Aquinas.

The idea of living with Howie finally helped convince my aunt, because I wouldn't be out there alone. My brother Peter lived close to there, too, so I'd have a support system. There was still a lot to figure out. The big thing was that I had to save up money to move out there.

I took that summer off from basketball for the most part. That was only partially my choice.

At that time there was a program in Ontario called the Nike ID Camp, which would bring kids to this big camp there from all across the country. They would fly you down, and US schools would come up and watch these top Canadian prospects. Because it was so small, Newfoundland only got to send one boy and one girl. I was the obvious choice, and 51 out of 52 coaches voted for me to go. One provincial coach rallied against me.

He made the case that because I was moving to Ontario, I shouldn't get the Newfoundland spot. The only reason I was moving to Ontario was to get recruited by American schools. If I'd gone to this camp and got a scholarship offer, I could have just come back home and played my grade twelve season in Newfoundland. And by the time the camp happened, I would have only been a ten-minute drive down the 401 in Toronto. But they saw it his way, and so they sent his son from Newfoundland instead.

Between that and needing to save up, I decided not to play with the Newfoundland team that summer. I wanted to focus on fishing with my uncle and making enough money to fly to Toronto and live with Howie. Uncle Junior did everything he could to help me pay for the plane ticket, too, and I was back to cutting the tongues out of cod to sell them for eighty cents a pound. I fished and worked all summer.

Once I had enough money, I flew out to Toronto and worked some more. Howie was a house framer, and he was able to get me work as a labourer on his job sites, and that paid pretty well for a high school kid. That gave me enough money to buy the uniforms—because St. Thomas Aquinas was a Catholic school—and to get new sneakers.

I did it. I had convinced my aunt, I had saved up enough money, I was going to play ball in Toronto, and I was going to get a scholarship. A lot of people still thought I was nuts, but I never put limitations on myself because I was a kid from Newfoundland, like others did. And one of the first things I did when I arrived in Toronto was get a tattoo on my arm. A basketball player is flying through the clouds, and the words "The sky is the limit" are written underneath.

* * * * *

In prison movies, everyone's told to show up the biggest guy in the yard and make a name for yourself. I took the same approach when I started at St. Thomas Aquinas.

I didn't know anyone yet, and I went hunting for a basketball game. I tried to figure out who the best player at the school was, and once I found that out, I wanted to play him one-on-one. That was Kamil Chmielewski. We went to an outdoor park across the street, and I got out there and just dominated him. We're still friends to this day, and I think because we were going to be on the same team, there were no hard feelings.

After that, everyone was talking about me, and the coaches were coming up to me. We'd reached out to the head coach, Anthony Cordeiro, ahead of time to explain the situation, so he knew who I was and had told some of the players. He was a really good coach. It was all setting up to be a great year.

All of a sudden, another bump in the road: the teachers went on strike. That year, eight school boards across Ontario were in a labour dispute. Some schools missed a couple of weeks of classes. The biggest impact on us was that there were no extracurriculars, which meant no basketball.

I was thinking, *What the hell happens now?* I hadn't come to Toronto for the education. I could get an education in Newfoundland. I had come to Toronto to get recruited. I wasn't going to let that stop me. So, I went to work.

Twenty years before highlight mixes on YouTube, I made my own mix tape. The great thing about a school that big, coming from Fatima Academy, was that there were a lot more resources. I went from a school of maybe 220 to a school with 2,500, and this massive school had a video room and all this tech equipment. I put together a highlight package of my games. Coach Pike in Newfoundland had taped some games, including my final game when we won the championship, and I planned to get a friend to come outside and use the camcorder to tape me dribbling and taking jumpers and dunking.

The teachers were really good about helping me out and letting me make my tapes. I would spend a free period or my lunch hour putting a tape together, and then I could copy that onto five or six tapes at a time. I'd set those up, go to class, come back to check on them later, and put on five more. The guidance counsellor got me the addresses for all of the Division I schools in the US, and I started mailing these tapes out. It took a few weeks of this to get them all done. I must have sent out at least 100 tapes. The last of the money I had from working all summer went to postage.

The tapes worked to some degree. I had Bradley, Creighton, Notre Dame, and Davidson all interested, and some other schools. Those are all fairly well-known schools now that have had some great shooters come through, but they were smaller at the time. They were low mid-majors. I was just randomly picking college basketball schools for which I might be able to play for.

The issue was that they all wanted to see me play. I'd sent these videos, and they'd call me up and say, "Well, is there a game we can come watch?" And I'd have to say, "No, the teachers are on strike."

I kept being told by coaches that the strike would be over soon. I didn't know what to do. I considered leaving, but I'd made friends, met new coaches and teammates, put down a few roots, and I didn't want to start over again. Every day people were telling me they were going to come off strike, and I believed them, so I kept waiting. The transfer deadline passed, and I was stuck.

It was frustrating. This was the whole reason I had moved away from my family and from Mandy. I got home only twice the whole year because it was so expensive to fly to Newfoundland. I'd go home, and it was hard to go back. I was there chasing a dream, the teachers were on strike, and I was calling home, missing people, and I was seeing my old team playing. I was thinking, *What am I doing?* At one point I was really close to just going back home. I figured I'd go home, finish the year, and then just go to Memorial University of Newfoundland or something. I chose to tough it out and keep waiting and trying.

We ended up hosting one tournament at our school at the end of the year where I played three games. That was it. That was my whole senior season at St. Thomas Aquinas. It really messed up my whole year. I made this huge move to Ontario to play basketball, and I couldn't play basketball because of a strike. I couldn't catch a break.

* * * * *

I spent that year getting a game of basketball wherever I could. In 1998, the Amateur Athletic Union (AAU) circuit wasn't nearly as developed as it is today, so there wasn't a way to jump on a team like that full-time to replace my high school ball. I'd just take a game whenever anyone asked, and because I came in with a bit of buzz, coaches and the people running those teams would invite me out. I was a basketball mutt that year, bouncing between teams and tournaments with no team of my own.

At first I would jump on with other high school teams for pre-tournaments. I was allowed to do that because the season hadn't started yet and these weren't official games.

I met Chris Van Zyl through one of the weightlifting coaches at St. Thomas Aquinas. The coach knew I was looking for games, and he knew a guy who was in the basketball community through one of their wives. Chris wasn't a coach, but he was up on the Toronto basketball scene.

We developed a relationship, and I trusted him pretty quickly. Sometimes I think the way I grew up hurt me a lot, in the sense that I grew up trusting everyone around me. I was very trusting, and so later, when I got away and was up in Ontario, and especially when agents started entering the mix later, I assumed the best of everyone. I grew up not locking my doors, with neighbours chipping in to send me and my brothers to camps or tournaments. And then I went away, and it was a whole different animal. People have their own motivations for helping you, maybe not intentionally, but it's a dog-eat-dog world, and I was naive to that for many years.

Chris was very good in many ways, especially that first year. He was in his late twenties, and he was trying to get his project, a precursor to an AAU team, Prep Stars Canada, off the ground. He knew everyone and where to find games, and he was really helpful driving me around and talking basketball with me, helping me learn the scene and find good competition to play against. We'd just go down and have a pickup game, and that's what it was.

There was definitely an adjustment to playing in Toronto. One of the first games we found was down at Jane and Finch, a notoriously rough part of town. I grew up in small-town Newfoundland, and now I was down in one of the toughest neighbourhoods in Canada. There were metal detectors when I entered the gym. Even my coaches were telling me not to speak—making sure I didn't trash-talk.

Before we tipped off, one of my teammates, whom I had just met, asked me, "Can you hang, Ghost?" The whole team was calling me Ghost because I was the only white player on the team. I'm not going to lie, I was a little scared. I didn't say anything, just kept my head down.

A couple plays into the game, I got the ball on the side of the floor. I used to do this little shake move. I'd shake quickly and then take off toward the net. I did that, and there was a seven-footer waiting in the paint. I dunked on him so hard the place went up. I mean, they knocked chairs over onto the floor, and teammates were picking me up. The whole game came to a stop. I'd never made a dunk like that in a game before. None of these people knew who I was, and I just shut the gym down.

We'd play pickup at Sheridan College, too. I was playing pretty much every day, and playing against those college players when you're in high school forces you to up your game. The quality of competition and the quality of the facilities was a big change. I went from playing once a week in a gym and the rest of my time on the pavement outside to playing in real games on real courts all the time.

On top of that, there were these AAU teams and tournaments Chris would get me involved with. He ran a tournament called the North American Invitational, which was a pretty big deal at the time. I played with Westwood, another Toronto high school. It was in down-town Toronto, and there were some big names playing. DerMarr Johnson was there, and he'd go on to be a consensus All-American. IMG Academy and Virginia Prep were there, too, so there were some really good teams.

That helped draw in a lot of American colleges, which was the first time a lot of those schools got to see me in person. In the first game of the tournament, I scored twenty-eight points. That caught every-one's attention. Everybody was like, "Who's this guy?" It was tougher after that, because nobody would pass me the ball. In a tournament like that, with schools and scouts on hand, everybody wants to shine.

Everybody's trying to get noticed and get a scholarship. And then you factor in that I wasn't even one of their teammates, so they froze me out a bit. I still averaged twenty points for the tournament, but I had to do a lot of rebounding to get touches and go Coast to Coast or hunt my own shots.

We did Adidas Prep Stars after that. Wayne Dawkins, who runs Phase 1 Academy now, was running that event. Denham Brown, who was a few years younger than me, was involved. I was on a team with a couple of players they'd brought in from Africa who would go on to play in the NCAA and overseas. They were big-time players, but they didn't speak much English. So, when I'd shoot, I'd have to tell them it was a shot. I'd scream out, "Shot!" Otherwise, they'd go up and dunk everything, because they could, and get called for offensive goaltending. We had a hell of a team.

It was a bit surreal to be bouncing around teams and events. I'd missed the Nike ID Camp, I'd skipped playing for Newfoundland, and then the teachers went on strike, so, for the first time, basketball had been taken away from me. Now I was playing again. I was playing against better competition, I was working out with weights for the first time, and I felt like I was getting better every game. Even when these big schools would come up, I was never star-struck, I was always just like, "What's next? What do I have to do?"

* * * * *

At the end of the year, I still didn't have any scholarship offers. That late in the game, it looked bleak because so many of the scholarships were already filled. Syracuse was all over me after the North American

Invitational, but they didn't have any scholarships available. My plan was to do a year of prep school at a place in Pennsylvania they had lined up, then go to Syracuse the following year.

In July, Chris took a van full of kids down to the US for some summer events. I hadn't been invited to any of the marquee prospect events, but I averaged thirty-two points in a New York City prep tournament, and then played really well at the Atlantic Cape Camp in New Jersey. I was named MVP of the camp and played in the camp's all-star game. The ABCD Camp was a bigger deal, and that was taking place in New York at the time. Since it was close, a bunch of coaches were able to leave that camp and come to New Jersey for our all-star game.

I tore that game up. After that, I had more than a dozen scholarship offers.

I was going to prep school. I'd made up my mind. Syracuse's reputation was stellar, my academics were in order, and there were no more hurdles to clear. But the paperwork was late to arrive, and all of a sudden I had more offers. Davidson and Creighton made their pitches, and I listened.

Hawaii was the most aggressive in its pursuit. Scott Rigot, their assistant coach, was recruiting me hard. He came up and found me at the Atlantic Cape Camp, and then once I was back in Toronto, working out, he came and visited me there, too. He even came out to Newfoundland and met Mandy and Aunt Betty after all of the camps wrapped up.

While he was out there, my younger brother Michael and I were playing ball. My brother was extremely talented. More talented than me, for sure. He just didn't have the same passion for basketball that I did. At the time, Coach Rigot was watching us shoot on the road, and he told me, "He'll be ten times better than what you are."

Coach Rigot and Chris met a lot. Chris was the only person I had helping me with all of this. I didn't have a support staff when it came to actual basketball decisions. My family was great and supportive, but none of us had gone through this before or had a basketball background, so nobody knew what was going on. My thinking was simple: I had ten or fifteen schools interested in me, so I thought let's pick one and figure it out.

When Hawaii asked me to come for a visit, it was a no-brainer. Even if I didn't think I would end up playing there, I told my brothers and Mandy, "Listen, I'm going to Hawaii, because it's Hawaii and I'll probably never have a chance to go there again."

Bernie Fine, the assistant at Syracuse who had been recruiting me, heard I was going to visit. He called and said, "Whatever you do, don't sign when you go to Hawaii." The schools and coaches tell you everything you want to hear when you go on those visits, and Hawaii is Hawaii, so I think everyone was a little worried I'd love it there and stay. They were right to worry.

Looking back, going to prep school and then going to a major program might have been my best route. I didn't know at the time. At that point I was focusing on trying to get a free education and play ball. Later, I realized that if the NBA was my goal, I shouldn't have gone to Hawaii. People would never see me. We could be a top twenty-five team, but for the most part scouts would only see me on the road and at tournaments. There's a credibility factor to the Atlantic Coast Conference (ACC), too. It's a lot different going into Cameron and dropping thirty against Duke versus putting up thirty-three against Fresno State. When I did that in Fresno State, everybody was asking, "Who is this kid?" and then they didn't see me again.

Hawaii wined and dined me. The coach, Riley Wallace, wasn't normally big on freshmen. He liked to build his team with junior college players and transfers so there was a bit more experience. But it was late in the summer, and they had a scholarship slot left. They'd already signed Phil Martin, too, so I'd have another Canadian there. They put on the full press. They took me out on this amazing yacht with a glass bottom where you could see all the fish below. They took me to all the best restaurants. I went to the gym and worked out and met all of the players. I was wowed. They told me everything I wanted to hear.

I signed while I was on the visit.

By then, Syracuse had figured it might be over. They'd managed to get all the paperwork done with the prep school, but it was too late. Coach Fine congratulated me, and we would stay in touch over the next couple of years.

Everybody at home was supportive. Coming from Newfoundland, it didn't make a lot of difference whether I'd be in Syracuse or Pennsylvania or Hawaii. I wasn't going to get to go home much. I'd been away from Mandy for a year and we managed, and I'd be able to come home in the summers and help Uncle Junior with the catch. Everyone had my back.

I accomplished goal number one. I was about to take a huge step, about to hop from one island to another.

5

FROM AWAY. HAWAII FRESHMAN YEAR.

THE DISTANCE FROM PATRICK'S COVE, Newfoundland, to Honolulu is just short of 10,000 kilometres. A direct flight from St. John's, if you could ever find one, would take nearly twelve hours. It's not exactly the other side of the world, but it may as well be.

The two places have more in common than you might think. I found on my initial visit that people in Hawaii were a lot like people in Newfoundland. It was one of the reasons I committed. Everyone was friendly, kind, and very caring. Over the years, my initial impressions proved correct. It was a lot like being home.

But the islands obviously had their differences. It took people time to get used to my accent. And Newfies have their own slang, so people thought I talked weird at first. We say "b'y" a lot, which is kind of just a stand-in word for "man" or "buddy." I ended a lot of sentences with ". . . right?" They called it fisherman's slang.

The biggest difference for me was the weather. It was amazing in Hawaii, and that was a welcome change. Honolulu is beautiful, one of the nicest places in the world. My dorm room was on the fifteenth floor. Looking out my window, I could see downtown Honolulu and the Pacific Ocean past Waikiki.

The culture was beautiful, too. The food was delicious, and I'll never forget experiencing the local rituals and festivals. The people were terrific. I think sometimes in life it's easy not to realize how special something is until it's over. Looking back on Hawaii, it was one of the most formative experiences of my life. I was truly lucky to go to school there, and I have basketball to thank.

One of the more difficult adjustments for me was getting used to Hawaii's laid-back culture. In that sense, it's another planet compared to Newfoundland. For one thing, everyone's late all the time. But I learned about "island time" and got used to life on a new island. I was focused on myself—my work in the gym, my goals—and I learned to adjust.

Honolulu had a different pace to life. It was relaxing. I spent a lot of time on the beach with my teammates. We surfed a lot. I was with a good group of guys—I was lucky in that sense, too. It made the adjustment easier. I learned that I loved the camaraderie of sports from an early age, and I loved being on a team.

I developed a reputation as a bit of a prankster. Every team has a guy or two who wears that hat, but people never expected it from me because I was so businesslike in my approach to basketball. But we had a lot of downtime, and it was a good way for me to balance myself out. When I was on the floor, only the game mattered, but off the floor, once I got comfortable, and once people got to know me better, I found the role suited me, and it stuck with me through the rest of my professional career.

Looking back, I did some things in Hawaii that probably could have gotten me expelled. Especially with Phil Martin, another freshman who also redshirted like me. We would get into trouble throwing cherry bomb firecrackers or playing pranks around the dorms. We were young and had tons of downtime. What do you expect?

The pranks played into one of my issues—I was restless. One of my teammates was quoted in an article saying I was "a little bit nuts and a bit wild," and I can see where he was coming from.

My restlessness showed itself in my hair, too. That's when I began experimenting with different looks and styles. I already looked like a surfer, or at least people told me so, and I leaned into it with shaggy, bleached blond hair. Other times I wore cornrows, shaved my head, or sported big sideburns.

Two distinctively different hairstyles Carl English sported during his years at the University of Hawaii.

The reason I was always trying weird stuff was that Lance Takaki, who was a walk-on for us and became a really close friend of mine, knew these ladies who taught hairdressing and were big fans of the team. Their names were Mitsy and Maya. On Thursday nights, Mitsy and Maya would have some of the guys from the team come in as guinea pigs. Phil, Lance, and I, and another guy named Mark Campbell would go in, and the students would work on our hair. We'd get our hair done for free, so I was willing to let them try whatever they wanted. And the teachers would demonstrate on us, so it usually turned out well. Or so I thought, at the time.

Those are the kind of things that help bond you with your teammates. They were all calling me C-Money once I started doing the weird things with my hair. I grew pretty close with Lance and Phil and another walk-on named Ryan Holiday.

Those connections were really important, because that first year was really rough for me.

* * * * *

Hawaii was incredible, but it wasn't home. I was six and a half time zones away from Mandy and my family, and I felt isolated. Visits back to Newfoundland were few and far between. Despite my new teammates, I was lonely.

Throughout my life, I always had basketball to turn to. No matter what was going on, basketball was my outlet. Now, for the first time, basketball was becoming a cause of frustration.

Coach Wallace was old-school. He was a good coach but hard on his players, especially freshmen. It was no secret he preferred junior college transfers. They brought more experience and, in his mind, were readier to contribute. I wasn't starting at the very bottom—I felt like I was starting in the parking lot. I told myself I'd be fine. I was on a scholarship, I was athletic, I could shoot, score, and I was a fighter. I would earn Coach Wallace's trust.

Then came ankle problems. Looking back, I realized running constantly with ankle weights and my homemade Jumpsoles wasn't the best for my ankles—in fact, they hurt more than they helped. Almost as soon as I got to Hawaii, I began to twist my left ankle repeatedly. I wore a brace, but it kept happening.

I played in a handful of pre-season games and then got into two games for garbage time in November. I scored a basket in both of them. It's hard to tell in pre-season and those small minutes, but I played okay. I wasn't star-struck or anything like that. I wasn't a typical freshman. The ankle kept bothering me, though.

Coach Rigot pulled me aside and suggested I tell Coach Wallace. He told me, "Go to the head coach, tell him everything that's going on with your ankle, and tell him you want to redshirt." I'd only played two official games, so I was still eligible for a medical redshirt. His thinking was that I wasn't going to play much as a freshman, anyway, so if we could get the ankle taken care of, I could use the year to get bigger and stronger. Phil was going to redshirt as well, and it would be a little easier for both of us, as redshirt Canadian roommates, if we were going through it together.

I told the coaches I'd do the surgery if they helped me fly home for Christmas so I could see my family.

That was a big ask. Life as a student-athlete in the NCAA was restrictive. I had no money, especially as a Canadian student. I was technically an international student, so I wasn't eligible for the Pell Grants that American students are getting. My scholarship provided $150 a month to live on. I had a meal card and my dorm was covered, but if I didn't like the food or wanted to go do something, the only bit of money in my pocket was that $150. If I went out and bought a pair of Jordans, I wouldn't have money for the rest of the month. If I didn't balance my money well, things would get tough.

I didn't really have time to work, either, because we had our basketball schedule and all of our courses, and we had to maintain certain standards to keep our scholarships. I'd do odd jobs for cash here and there.

There were some big boosters of the program who would help us if we needed it. The Gaty, Chung, and Kam families were all great to us and would have a few players over for dinners or take us tailgating to the football games. Ron Yee was another. He would do a lot of building projects, and I'd work as a labourer. There were some other people who would give us a bit of work, but nothing major, just enough to keep us in shoes and phone cards.

The worst part was that we couldn't use the school phones. I realize how silly that sounds, but using a school phone to call your family at home was considered a violation as a student-athlete. I couldn't call home, because they would check phone bills. As athletes, we could make millions of dollars for the school and for the NCAA, but we couldn't call our loved ones. So much of how the NCAA treated student-athletes defied common sense. *Are you kidding me right now?* was a common thought I had.

We used to sneak into the media room at the arena after practice to use the phones. We'd go and check to see if they left the doors unlocked the last time media were there, and if it was unlocked, we'd go in and make calls. The coaches would find out, and they'd call us and tell us we couldn't do that. But they would help, too. There were a certain number of times a coach could call a player's family and let them know how they were doing. The assistants, Bob Nash, Jackson

Wheeler, and Scott Rigot, would leave the room for a bit and tell us not to use the phone in a sort of "wink, wink" way.

I was a world away from Mandy and my family, I was dealing with not playing and with my ankle, and I was trying to decide on surgery, and I couldn't even call home. Something as simple as communicating with my family was so hard. I wanted to talk to them. I was down and out. I wanted to hear Mandy's voice. The school had Internet, but nobody back home had it or email. Mandy was racking up $300 and $400 in phone bills, and a lot of what little money I had was spent on phone cards.

The school was able to arrange to send me home for Christmas. I was about to have surgery for the first time.

* * * * *

I had the surgery on December 11. The doctors went in with a scope and cleaned everything up. They had to reattach a few ligaments and clean up some little pieces of bone. I'd have to wear a walking boot for six to eight weeks to let it all heal and then rehab my way back.

I couldn't stay off the court, even when I was just out of surgery. The cast they put me in had blocks at the bottom to help me walk around, which meant I could also put up shots in the gym. The coaches would yell at me to get off my ankle, but I just couldn't stay away.

Two days after the cast came off, I was dunking. Let's just say that when I was having ankle surgeries later, in 2010 and 2019, I didn't respond quite as fast.

Rehabbing was tough, but the one nice thing about redshirting was that it gave me a target. I knew I wouldn't be back that season, so all of my energy could go into getting ready to be as good as possible that next year. This was really the first time I was doing a weights program, and between the start of my first year and my second year, I added about twenty-five pounds. I'd come in a little scrawny, but now I was lean and mean.

I had a lot of time to focus on my game while I was hurt. I kept shooting, despite the boot. I was in the gym every day. The only way I knew to respond to blocks on my path was to work even harder to overcome them. A tough freshman year and an ankle injury weren't going to stop me.

The whole process gave me a lot of confidence. I healed pretty quickly, and then I was allowed to rejoin practices on the scout team. In practices, you have your starters and your second unit, and then you have your scout team of guys who don't play much, who try to help get the main guys ready for each opponent. The coaches would teach us some of the next opponent's plays, and we'd run them so our guys could get used to seeing them and defending them.

Everyone started to see my potential when I got on these scout teams, because I was getting all of these reps against our starters. I could shoot as much as I want, and I was kicking their asses. The first and second teams had trouble stopping me. *Who's this redshirt?* The buzz surrounding our team started building a little bit. Coach Wallace still doesn't care much for freshmen, but I was hoping this would start winning him over for next year.

But first, I had to go home and help with the catch.

6

Loss. Uncle Junior.

EVERY FISHING SEASON, FISHING FAMILIES in Newfound-land are given a quota. That's the amount the government sets out each year that you're allowed to catch of each type of fish. How comfortable a family will be for the year depends on the price of fish and how close they can get to their quota.

In the summer of 2000, I came home from Hawaii to help Uncle Junior and my cousin Howie catch our family's quota, just like I'd done before I left. Those summers were always a taste of what life would be like if I wasn't playing basketball. Everyone I knew was a fisher person, so it all seemed like the most normal thing in the world.

Even as a nineteen-year-old, it was nothing new to be up at four thirty in the morning, depending on the weather, and getting right to work. Because I was on the boat all day, I'd have to wear these big green rubber overalls, like rubber boots for your whole body. I would handle the lines and the jiggers, haul in the nets, gut and ice the fish, and then we'd go home and do it all again the next day.

Uncle Junior couldn't do much on his own because of a heart condition. He'd get us up in the morning and then help with what he could and watch over the whole process. And we couldn't complain because he never complained, and it was a lot harder for him at that point than it was for us. I hate fishing. I hate it! But I couldn't complain. And if I did, Uncle Junior would be all over me, making fun of me if I complained about the cold or the wet or the hours. I also knew how much the family relied on us catching our quota.

On the morning of June 3, we caught about 1,000 pounds of cod. It was a harsh day. The Newfoundland summer is short, and it's sandwiched between rainy seasons. There was a lot of rain, and the temperature only got up to nine degrees. It wasn't an outlier, but it was miserable.

Uncle Junior started complaining about being cold.

Howie and I were pretty alarmed, because he never complained. I'd never seen him ask to come in off the boat before we'd filled our haul for the day or the sun was going down. For Uncle Junior to say something like that, he must have been feeling awful.

We started pulling in all of our lines and nets and headed back in. Once we got to the wharf, we started unloading the catch. Normally, Uncle Junior would sit in the boat and make sure everything was going smoothly since he couldn't help.

This time, he got up on the wharf. He'd never gotten up on the wharf before.

We were unloading, and I heard him call my name. It was just a whisper. "Carl." I can still hear his voice, throaty and strained. I could hear the air come out of him.

I knew his heart had stopped. I looked up, and Uncle Junior collapsed.

There wasn't anything I could do. Because of his condition, Howie and I didn't really want to go at him ourselves. We didn't know what we were supposed to do, so we called the ambulance. I was standing there waiting, my world collapsing. I could still hear air releasing from his body in these strained exhales. I knew he was dead, and I was in shock. I was thinking, *Holy . . . is this really happening?* The world felt like it was spinning.

Once the ambulance got there, nothing was working. CPR wasn't working. There was no pulse. With Uncle Junior's heart the way it was, I already knew. Howie and I raced home to get changed out of our fishing gear, and someone called ahead to tell Aunt Betty. By the time we all got to the hospital, he had been pronounced dead.

It was devastating to see. I had watched my parents catch on fire as a child, but a lot of those memories were repressed. My parents died later, at the hospital. I'd never seen someone die before, and now I had watched the person closest to me in the entire world die. I felt so helpless. All of the questions I felt as a child came rushing back to me. At first it was, "What the hell is going on?" Then it was, "Why me? Why us? Why again?" I was questioning faith. I was questioning everything.

I lost my parents at such an early age that it didn't really affect me until I got older. I found for a long time my brothers and I were defined by the loss of our parents, at least until we made our own lives and went down our own paths. It shaped who we were. It was a chapter that made us stronger and developed our character, and we had to hope it made us better people rather than let it destroy us. In dealing with tragedy, you can either let it destroy you or rise above it. My attitude was always to let it make me stronger and help me.

With Uncle Junior, it was different.

It was just, boom, he dropped dead in front of me. I was lost. I didn't understand why it was happening and why this was happening to me, again. Most people don't lose a parent until later on in life, and I'd lost three by the time I was a teenager. I'd lost two fathers in one lifetime. My whole childhood, Uncle Junior and I had been hand in hand because of his disability and because I had lost my parents. There aren't enough words to explain what Uncle Junior meant to me. It turned my whole life upside down.

I thought I was finally at a place where a lot of my trials were ready to reward me. I had a scholarship, basketball was good, I was healthy again, and I was home with my family for the summer. Uncle Junior had helped make so much of that possible. I always want to share my successes with the people that were closest to me. It's always been something that's driven me. He was a huge part of my life and my most important supporter, and this whole time I'd thought I would get to share whatever I accomplished with him. And now this.

I was a wreck at the funeral. The church was packed, and everyone was looking at me and seeing how I was doing, a lot like my parents' funeral. I wasn't nearly as strong or quiet this time. I didn't take cues from my brothers. I felt my whole world crashing, and I let it show.

When a casket is closed, that's the end of it. *He's gone now.* When they closed Uncle Junior's, I broke down and couldn't stop crying. My brother Kevin was holding me, and my brothers had to carry me out of the church. It was the lowest point of my life.

It took me a long time to start to recover. Eventually, I'd come to know Uncle Junior was still my biggest fan, looking down on me. When I got my parents' faces tattooed on my back, his was right there with them. But I held on to the grief for a long time. He meant everything to me, and I'd already lost so much. I was so angry and incredibly sad.

What was I supposed to do now?

7

RISE. HAWAII, YEARS TWO TO FOUR.

WHEN UNCLE JUNIOR DIED, I was lost. My whole life, the only thing I had known to do in those situations was turn to basketball. So, that's what I did.

That summer was my first time playing for the Canadian national program. I'd been invited to the under-twenty-one team for the Championship of the Americas for Young Men. I knew Uncle Junior would want me to play. He would have wanted me to do it, to be able to focus on basketball.

It became my way out again. It was my way of dealing with the tragedy. Everyone around me was trying to comfort me, and my response was, "No, let's do the next thing, let's go play ball and block it all out." I wanted to use it to motivate me and try to get stronger again, like I had with the loss of my parents.

I went to play for Team Canada in Brazil. The competition there was strong, similar to what the University Games are now. I started on that team and played well. My ankle felt great, which was encouraging. It wasn't so much about the performance for me, though. I felt that playing with Canada allowed me to deal with Uncle Junior's passing. It took me out of the situation.

It was the same when I returned to Hawaii. Focusing on basketball allowed me to deal with the loss every day and slowly start to overcome it. Everyone develops their own way of handling tragedy when it hits them, and basketball was my coping mechanism. I always felt that I was free when I was on the court. I feel that way to this day—I could lock in to the pressure of the game, the moments, the smell of the ball, the bounce, everything. Blocking out everything I was feeling was possible as I focused on the task at hand. I don't know if that was the best way to recover, but it was the only thing that allowed me to be successful.

In fact, it was the only thing that allowed me to function at all. Losing family members at such a young age hardens you. My relationship with Uncle Junior was special, and basketball had become a part of it, so basketball was like my psychiatrist. It was my sanctuary.

* * * * *

I was back at the bottom for my second year at Hawaii, which was my true freshman year. Coach Wallace had recruited a few new players, and when there were new players, everyone was gunning to take someone else's job. I didn't have a job in the first place, so I had to work that much harder.

Having a year under my belt was helpful. I'd learned how to balance life as a student-athlete, and I felt good physically. I was bigger and stronger and more used to the college game.

My season got off to a fun start at our Midnight Ohana event, a season kickoff the team holds for fans. There was an intra-squad scrimmage, and we'd have to do skits and interact with the fans. It was always a fun night.

There was also a dunk contest. Lance Takaki, the walk-on who had the hairdressing hookup, was five foot four and made for a good dunk partner. I dunked over him to win that year's dunk contest. I cleared him with my legs spread out to the sides. The picture was in the local papers. I don't know if people there knew I could dunk like that yet, because I'd hardly played. They did after that.

I was playing well as we got ready for the season, too. Coach Wallace loved the junior college transfers because of their experience, so I had to fight for playing time early on. I played twenty-eight of thirty-one games that season, but I was coming off the bench, and my minutes were inconsistent. We hosted our annual Rainbow Classic in late December, and I had a big tournament. We made the finals and lost to Tennessee, who were in the top ten in the country at the time. We'd played St. Louis in the semifinal, and I scored eight of our last ten points, including some big free throws down the stretch, and then I didn't play much in the final.

That was common that season. I started to feel like there was no momentum for me. I would do something good and think I was about to have my chance, but nothing carried over game to game.

At this point Chris knew I was frustrated, so he started talking with Bernie Fine at Syracuse again. We were curious about whether transferring was an option. I wanted to know what I could do in the summer if I still thought I wasn't a part of Coach Wallace's plans.

Sometimes coaches believe in certain players, and trust has to be developed. I understood that. What I didn't understand was how I was supposed to do it without getting a chance. I felt I was good enough to play—I was dominating in practice, and I put in all the extra time. My attitude was that at least I was getting better, and if I transferred at the end of the year, so be it.

Things turned around mid-season. I'd been out playing the guards ahead of me at practice every day. I was still on the scout team some-times, and there was one practice where I'd hit a bunch of threes in a row. Coach Wallace told the first team, "If he hits another three, every one of you guys are running for the rest of practice." The guys were begging me not to shoot it. Around that same time, one of our point guards got hurt.

Coach Wallace wasn't aware that I intended to transfer, but now he didn't have much of a choice other than to play me. One of our se-niors, Nerijus Puida, talked to Coach Wallace and told him to give me a chance, which I really appreciated. The guys knew our season was teetering. We were fighting for a playoff spot in the Western Athletic Conference (WAC), and I was better than our other guard options.

Coach Wallace finally relented and started playing me more. I was still coming off the bench, but my role was bigger, the minutes were more consistent, and I had more responsibility. I was tearing it up. My averages were still nothing special because I'd barely played earlier in the year, but I was putting up thirteen or fourteen points and five or six assists most nights, playing as a big point guard instead of a combo guard.

We finished 8-8 in conference play, which was good enough for the No. 5 seed in our conference tournament. We got to the semifinal and beat Fresno State, which was a big upset. They were a top twenty-five team and were expected to win our conference. We'd picked up steam late, but we weren't expected to make this deep a run.

We drew Tulsa in the finals and were the underdog again. I was having my best game of the season. I'd scored sixteen points off the bench heading into the final few plays. We were down two in the final seconds. That's when Coach Wallace drew up the play for Predraeg Savović, which ended up with the ball in my hands. I tied the game, then scored seven more points in overtime to win it.

Hawaii had only been to the NCAA Tournament twice before and hadn't been since 1994. For us to come back like that late in the year and win the WAC as a No. 5 seed was wild! It was huge for the school, and it was huge for me. I had put up forty-four points, sixteen rebounds, and eleven assists across the three games and scored a career-high twenty-five in the final. I won MVP of the WAC Tournament, which caught a lot of people by surprise. The general response was, "Who is this guy who averaged five points?"

The thing I remember most is Jerry Tarkanian comparing me to a young Jerry West on the broadcast. Coach Tark saying something like that about you gets people to take notice.

* * * * *

My whole college career skyrocketed from there. It was instant stardom.

Making March Madness as a mid-major, let alone when you're a low seed in your own conference, gets networks to take notice. The NCAA and the broadcasts looked for stories they could push during the tournament, and someone like me, going from barely playing to being tournament MVP, especially coming from where I came from and with my backstory, made for an obvious choice. CBS sent a crew to Newfoundland to talk to my brothers and to talk about my parents. The games were broadcast all across the country, and a lot of people got to see me for the first time.

I was becoming somebody as a prospect. I knew inside all along who I was and what I could do, but six weeks before that, I was trying to transfer. After we made the tournament and I broke out, my thinking became, *Okay, I'm here now.*

We drew a No. 12 seed and played Syracuse in the first round, which was fitting. We struggled with their zone for a lot of the game but managed to keep it close. We lost 79-69, which was a respectable showing for a program our size against a school like Syracuse.

The whole process was amazing. When we went back to school after that, everything changed. We were the big team on campus. Everyone was behind us. It helped the program, too, because it was their first time making the tournament in a few years, and potential recruits could see the school. It brings in a lot of money, too, so the school was obviously really happy with us.

Even when I went home to Newfoundland in the summer, people started to recognize me more. Mandy would always notice it. People would be looking at us if we were in St. John's, and I wasn't hard to spot because I was fix foot five at this point and had the bleached blond surfer hair.

Our success helped a lot back on campus the next year, too, because everyone wanted to keep supporting the program and the players however they could.

The boosters helped bring my younger brother, Michael, out to Hawaii. Michael was entering grade twelve, and the boosters helped get him into Punahou, an exclusive private school where tuition was more expensive than my college scholarship. The people at the program wanted to do as much as they could to support me because I'd become an integral part of the program, and bringing Michael out was a great way to make me happy and more comfortable.

Michael stayed with Al Kam, his wife, and his brother Allan. He came to the university every day after school to spend time with me, and one of the Kams would pick him up later. It was a great chapter. It gave me a lot more confidence, having someone I was so close with nearby.

Initially, Michael had been excited to come. The plan was for him to finish high school at Punahou and then hopefully earn a basketball scholarship at Hawaii. After a couple of months, Michael decided he wanted to go back to Newfoundland. He was struggling with being away, which I understood. As his older brother, I wanted to get him to stick it out, because I knew it was a good path for him to get a scholarship and a degree, but I also wanted to be supportive of him.

The boosters also helped me land a job. There was a great family named Merriman, Wally and his son John, who were big supporters of the team and ran a testing and inspection company at which I could work.

You might think a job for a student-athlete was just a cover-up for guys getting a little bit of money, but the Merrimans were strict. I actually had to work, and we filled out all the proper forms, because the NCAA tracked all of those things closely. My job title was Engineer Technician. I even had it on a business card. My role was to measure the strength of different concrete pours before they went into buildings. I'd have to take samples of each pour, pour them into cylinders, put them into different water baths, then take them out and see how much intensity they could withstand before they cracked. I'd have to work at least once or twice a week, and because of my schedule, sometimes I had to be in there at five in the morning before class.

I had to make sure I got my hours in to qualify for the perks that other employees got. As long as I hit my hours, the job entitled me to a car and a phone. That made life so much easier. Having a bit more walking-around money goes a long way when you're used to $150 a month. I could call home more, which made things easier with Mandy and made it easier to deal with a bad day or a tough practice.

My hope was that the bad days would be less frequent in the year to come.

* * * * *

The tournament didn't do anything other than keep motivating me. I always tried to stay humble and stay hungry for what was next. Once we made a tournament appearance, for me it was, "What are we doing next? How are we getting better?"

I'd gone home to help Howie with the fishing for the summer, so I had to stagger all of my workouts around that. That was definitely a drain on my development. My workouts were at strange times because I had to spend most of the day fishing. When I did get to play, the players I went up against weren't on the same level. I'd be letting guys do whatever they wanted to try to stop me or make it competitive, as long as they didn't hurt me.

It helped in terms of finishing through contact and playing physical, but really I was at a level where I should have been training in Los Angeles with NBA guys or at IMG Academy. Those things cost money, and my family had to be my first priority, especially after Uncle Junior's death. I always felt coming home was a good way to stay grounded in the summers. I could come home and refresh, train every day, and then go back and attack the next year with a vengeance. That was my approach every off-season.

There were high hopes for that year. We had a lot of guys returning, and even in the first few practices, we could tell we were better. The tough part that year was getting teams who would come out to play us. There weren't as many big teams that came out to the Rainbow Classic. Georgia was the biggest, and we beat them in the final. The thing with Hawaii was that teams loved playing there when we were bad. It was a fun trip for them. When we were good, it was risky to come out to Hawaii as a higher-ranked team and lose. The teams still treated a trip to Hawaii like it was a vacation, and for us those were huge games, so there was a difference in motivation. The bigger programs worried that coming to play us was going to kill their rating percentage index (RPI) ratings.

Even without big-name opponents, we finished that year ranked in the top twenty-five. We were 27-5 and blew everyone out in the WAC tournament to qualify for the NCAA Tournament again. I averaged 15.5 points, 5.1 rebounds, 3.3 assists, and shot 39.9 per cent from three. Predraeg Savović had been suspended for part of the season, so I took on the role as our main scorer and made all-WAC second team. I had some monster games on the road and a really strong WAC tournament, which was always important because scouts rarely came to Hawaii. I was starting to get noticed.

In February, we went to play Southern Methodist University (SMU) in Texas. Steve Nash was playing with the Dallas Mavericks and reached out to tell me he was going to come to our game. He wanted to talk to me about playing for the national team that summer. At first the guys didn't believe me. Nobody thought he was actually coming. And then he walked into the gym in his sweats, and all of my teammates went nuts. It was pretty crazy. We were this mid-major playing on the road, and an NBA All-Star was coming to watch us. I had a huge game that night, too—twenty-one points, nine rebounds, and five assists.

Buzz was building. In January, *Sports Illustrated* had written a big profile on our team, which everyone got really excited about, and CBC did a big TV feature on me back home. We had players from seven different countries, and it looked like we were going to make the tournament again, so outlets were giving us some love and telling our story when the tournament came around.

I thought with more buzz and with our second NCAA Tournament appearance, the bright lights would be a little easier to deal with. That wasn't the case. We were a No. 10 seed, so we got a more favourable draw than the year before. We were playing Xavier, who had David West and Romain Sato at the time. I felt we were better than them.

The stardom got to our guys. Playing in Hawaii, there were only a few camera crews because there were only a few stations. Playing in the tournament, there was national coverage, everybody's family was coming out—it was a major deal. For a lot of guys, that was the highlight of their career. That shot us in the foot. I think that's the advantage some of the bigger schools have in that environment. A team in the ACC like Duke or North Carolina is in the spotlight every day. The tournament is just another game. As a mid-major, going to the tournament is massive. It's an accomplishment all on its own.

We were the better team, but we lost our composure as that game went on. A couple of the guys argued with each other, and there was a blow-up at halftime. Everyone wanted a chance to shine a little bit, and guys didn't handle that well with the adrenaline flowing. We were playing well but imploded in the second half.

So, we were one-and-done again, and it was back to the drawing board. It's still an amazing year any time you make the tournament from a school like Hawaii. We got our rings, the boosters were happy, and everybody was excited.

But I wanted to advance and get better. I entered that summer the same way as usual, looking for a way to take the next step.

I regret not playing for the national team that summer. Steve Nash and Jay Triano, the coach at the time, really wanted me to go out for the 2002 World Championships. Canada went 0-3 there, and I felt like I could have helped. I felt like I missed a huge opportunity, too, to get to play with Steve at his peak and build a relationship with him.

It was a tough decision. Chris was in my ear telling me not to go. He thought I didn't need them and they needed me, and I don't think he understood the value of learning from a guy like Steve. The bigger factor was that Howie and I had to go home to fish. We had to catch enough cod so Aunt Betty could live comfortably for the year. Jay was interviewed about me that summer and joked that if I'd caught more fish, the team could have had me. It was the truth of the situation.

My family was my priority. If I had my time back, I would have found a way to play. People were starting to talk about me as a potential NBA player, and I was starting to pop up on draft boards, so it would have been helpful to have Steve's counsel. He'd been through the NBA and experienced the draft process. I wasn't so egotistical that I wouldn't be all ears around a guy like that. It was Steve Nash.

Even without playing for Canada, my stock was rising. I started letting myself think, *This could happen. If I continue to work, this could be a reality.* I had never really thought about being good enough to play in the NBA until that season. It was mostly just a dream. Once that became more realistic, that was all the motivation I needed. It became, for me, "Okay, what do I have to do now?"

I took it to another level my junior year. Savović had graduated, so I had an even bigger role. I averaged 19.6 points, shot 39.2 per cent on threes, and made all-WAC first team. The numbers got noticed—I was now the other team's primary focus on defence and was still scoring at that level, and I had some big games on the road.

There were more scouts out for those road games, and their draft experts were updating their mock drafts and mentioning me. Everyone was asking me about it. I can't imagine what it's like for kids now, because even back then I was being bombarded. We'd go on the road to play a good team like Fresno State, and our media guys would grab me and say, "Carl, man, there's twenty scouts here tonight." I didn't want to have a bad game on the road, because that scout might not see me again.

Sports Illustrated and ESPN both did profiles on me that winter. Due to how well I was playing and my upbringing, everyone wanted to tell my story. I was from a town of seventy people where I couldn't even get these magazines. It was unbelievable. There was a magazine cover with Yao Ming on it, and my name was in the corner. It was surreal.

Unfortunately, our team wasn't as strong that year. We lost to Tulsa in the semifinal of the WAC tournament, which meant no NCAA Tournament berth. We did the National Invitation Tournament (NIT) instead and made it to the second round.

Balancing school with being on the road was tougher down the stretch. Over the last five weeks of the season, we were at home briefly for two games to close out our conference schedule. It was so expensive to fly back and forth from Hawaii, we'd go to wherever we were playing and just wait to find out where we had to go next and then fly there. Essentially, we were on the road for five weeks during the time when we were trying to get ready for exams. We travelled with professors and did a lot of distance education and study halls during those trips. I couldn't let that side of things slip, because I had a timeline in mind.

I was a junior, but because I'd redshirted my first year, I was on track to graduate with a degree in sports management and a minor in kinesiology that spring. My wife is a kinesiologist and occupational therapist. She was doing her degree in Newfoundland, and we thought if we both had kinesiology and I had sports management, we'd be set up well for when I was done playing basketball.

I wanted to make sure I got that done and graduated on time in case I wanted to turn pro. I was third team Academic All-American with a 3.75 GPA and finished all of my credits. I still had a year of eligibility left, too, so I was thinking about doing a master's if I didn't enter the draft.

After the year I'd had, that was going to be a really tough decision.

8

HYPE. PRE-DRAFT PROCESS.

WHEN TALK STARTED THAT I was a potential NBA prospect, everybody had an opinion. After my junior year, there was a bit of a frenzy because I'd had such a good season and people considered me a potential draft pick, but I hadn't publicly declared yet. I hadn't even decided what I was doing.

It's good the Internet wasn't as big as it is now and I didn't have a smart phone back then. There was a lot of noise. Nobody around me had ever been through the process before, so I was trying to figure out what to do on my own. I didn't really know who to listen to.

Coach Wallace didn't want me to go pro. The big reason, obviously, was that we'd become a winning program. Phil Martin and I could both come back for our senior years and we'd be a strong team. We could be a monster and make another appearance in the tournament. He didn't want his best player to leave with a year of eligibility left. For a coach, a four-year run like we would have had could earn you a lot more money and security, and Coach Wallace deserved it. He'd been there twenty years, and the program was doing great.

The other reason he wanted me to stay was that he thought I was getting some bad advice. He told me and other people that I needed to come back. That might have hurt my stock a little bit, but he cared. My brother Peter came down to see me late that year, and Coach broke it down for him. He told Peter, "He's caught up. He's trusting some people. He should come back."

At the time I didn't feel like Coach Wallace was in my corner. Chris led me to believe that Coach Wallace wanted me back for selfish reasons. I trusted Chris. And because I trusted him, I believed everything he was telling me. I had no reason to think I couldn't trust Chris. I was a loyal person to a fault, and he'd done nothing to steer me wrong. So, I didn't really listen to what Coach Wallace was saying. He wasn't a part of the process for me.

One of the mistakes I made was not being truly honest with Coach Wallace during the process. I respected him a lot, and with that respect came fear. I didn't feel I could speak to him openly and freely. I feel like I misled him a bit. I knew deep down there was a good chance I wasn't coming back, and I didn't communicate that when I left that summer. It was a Catch-22, because I honestly wasn't sure yet what I was going to do.

When I finally decided, Coach Wallace was out on a recruiting trip. I announced with one of the assistant coaches that I would be exploring the NBA. Then the hype started building.

* * * * *

I left Hawaii and went back to Ontario as my base for the pre-draft process. I didn't even stay around for graduation. I finished my classes, graduated, and came back to get ready.

I did most of my training with Chris in Orangeville, just outside of Toronto. Jesse Tipping ran a facility in Orangeville that eventually became the Athlete Institute, which has had guys like Jamal Murray come through. At that time it was just a gym and a workout area that was freshly built. My brother Peter lived down the street and had been telling me about this beautiful new gym, so I stayed with Peter and went to the Orangeville gym with Chris to train.

Leandro Barbosa's agent reached out to see if I was interested in training with him to get ready for the draft. He ended up getting picked twenty-eighth, and he was a heck of a player. It might have been good to get to work out with him regularly and have someone of that calibre pushing me. It might have helped me get more exposure, too, working out with another potential first-round pick. Any time another agent or camp reached out, Chris thought we should stick with our small group in Orangeville, so we did that.

The first part of the draft process was the combine in Chicago. The league took our measurements and ran us through athletic testing, and most of the guys still participated in five-on-five games at that time. I had Kyle Korver on my team for those sessions, which was interesting, because teams would think of us in a similar group as shooters.

Coming out of the combine, my stock was strong. I was talked about in the twenty-to-forty range in the draft, which was pretty good, because that draft year was loaded. The 2003 draft had LeBron James, Dwyane Wade, Carmelo Anthony, and Chris Bosh. There was Darko Miličić, too, and they'd changed a rule for him so that international prospects could enter the draft a little earlier than before. The draft was heavy at the top, and it was expected to be fairly deep. I took being projected in the early second round as a positive.

Chris understood the power of the media before most people.

The next year, Chris had Ivan Chiriaev, a nineteen-year-old Russian kid, and they made this huge hype storm for him. They made him out to be the next Dirk Nowitzki. Then he had to actually work out for NBA scouts, and it fell apart. But Chris knew how to create buzz like that. With me being the rare Canadian to have a chance to get drafted, that was an easy story to sell. His whole approach was, "We've gotta attack the media. The media is the boost we need." That helped keep the buzz going.

I hadn't signed an agent yet, so Chris was handling everything. At that time you could do the combine and the pre-draft process and then pull out and return to school as long as you didn't hire an agent. This was where a relationship with Steve Nash would have been helpful, even if it was just to get connected with his agent, Bill Duffy, or hear about his experience with the draft cycle. Chris didn't know Duffy, so we didn't trust Duffy. All my trust was going into Chris.

Chris connected me with Harold Cipin, who was new to being an agent and had never represented a basketball player before. He wasn't a bad guy, but he had no connections or experience in the industry. If I had a seasoned vet like a Duffy or Andrew Vye, my agent later in my career, I would have received guidance through the whole process. I turned down a lot of big-time agents because Chris trusted Harold and I trusted Chris.

I also felt some loyalty to Harold. In my last year at Hawaii, Chris had been putting a little bit of extra money into my account. It wasn't much, about $1,500 spread out over a few seasons. To a college kid, that's a lot. An extra $150 every month was doubling what I got from my scholarship money. I didn't have any financial help from home— I had to work all summer to help Aunt Betty, and work during the school year for spending money—so that little bit of help was a big deal to me.

Looking back, it's hard to believe that $1,500 was enough to buy loyalty for these million-dollar decisions later. Chris told me the money was coming from an agent, and Chris was the middleman so that there wasn't a violation.

When it came time to pick an agent, Harold had been helping me out, and he was Chris's guy, so we went with him. I was naive about what Chris might be getting from it or what choosing a first-time agent over an experienced agent meant. I grew up knowing that everyone around me had my best interests at heart. It made me trust for the wrong reasons as I got older. I was new to the idea that people might be helping me out solely for themselves. Being so loyal hurt me a couple of times throughout my career.

Chris was such a strong influence on me because I had nobody else to help make that decision. Everyone was supportive, but for the actual basketball decision, I couldn't turn to Mandy, I couldn't turn to my brothers, and I felt I couldn't turn to Coach Wallace. I don't think I was alone in that experience, either. I think a lot of student-athletes hit that roadblock. It would have been different if I were a senior, because then I'd be done and everyone would be behind me. As an underclassman, some people wanted me to come back, and some people wanted me to go pro. I was twenty-two years old, my own man at that point, and I had to live by the decisions I made, but Chris was the only person I trusted, and he was really pushing me toward Harold.

Looking back on it, I'd have had to be an idiot to enter a draft that good with a year of eligibility left unless it were a sure thing. A good agent would have sat me down and said, "Carl, you're not entering the draft. This is the strongest draft class in NBA history. Let's go through the pre-draft process, get all of that experience, then go chill on the beach and work on your master's, and we'll enter the draft in 2004." I wasn't getting that kind of feedback. My path should have been crystal clear, but I didn't know if it was the right thing.

In hindsight, I wouldn't have stayed in. You never know what could have happened. I could have gone back as a senior and blown out my knee. But I look at the domino effect that not being drafted set off over the next few years, and it's hard not to ask, "What if?" If I did another year, put up good numbers again, was on the watch list for the John Wooden Award as the country's top player, made another tournament run, and then entered a much weaker draft class, who knows what could have happened?

It goes down as a lesson in being careful whom you trust. It's happened to so many kids that the NBA and the players' association have stepped in over time to do more to protect the players. There's more freedom in the pre-draft process and a lot more feedback before you have to make your choice. I didn't have those advantages to make the right decision.

Ultimately, we decided to go with Harold and stay in the draft.

* * * * *

After the combine, teams start bringing prospects in for pre-draft workouts. Over a couple of weeks, I flew all over the country to get in front of as many teams as possible. That was especially important for a player like me, who had a pretty wide projected draft range. I wanted to get in and impress in front of coaches and general managers, even if that meant spending the whole time exhausted from flying around so much.

I did thirteen workouts over sixteen days leading up to the draft. There was another catch in the process that helped make my decision to hire an agent—if you did pre-draft workouts with teams, you had to pay back all of the money for flights and hotels to go back to school. The teams were flying me first class, putting me in nice hotels, and covering my meals, and at the end I would have had to pay all of that back if I wanted to return to college. We're talking probably $75,000 that I would have had to pay to remain eligible. That helped me make the decision; once I was in, I was in.

The workout circuit was really cool, bouncing all over and getting to meet all of these NBA people. A couple of my best workouts were in Indiana, Minnesota, and Atlanta. Atlanta brought me in for a second workout. That's usually a good sign, so I skipped a workout with Cleveland to work out with Atlanta again. They ended up drafting Jason Kapono, so they were looking for shooters. I also did Denver, Seattle, Chicago, and both Los Angeles teams.

My workout in Miami was the one I remember most because of Wade. We were in the same workout, and I scored on him a few times early on. I started talking some smack to him, letting the adrenaline take over. The next time I got the ball, it seemed like he wasn't even trying. I blew by him and went up for a floater, and I swear, Wade almost pinned that thing to the shot clock. He came out of nowhere. He would end up being one of the best shot-blocking guards ever, and at that point he was in his physical prime. I guess I rubbed him the wrong way. He was the one talking trash the rest of the workout.

Another really fun workout was with the Raptors. Steve Nash was starting to reach the height of his game at that time, and Jamaal Magloire was in the NBA, and that was it for Canadians. I was the next up-and-comer, so the media was pretty crazy for the idea of me being picked by the Raptors. Glen Grunwald was the general manager, and they'd just hired Kevin O'Neill as head coach, so they were going through some changes and it was hard to tell what they might do.

All of the interviews and workouts with the Raptors went great. They were pretty honest with the press. They had the No. 4 pick, which they'd use on Bosh, and it was obvious they weren't going to take me there. I knew I wasn't a lottery pick, so that was fine. And then because of a trade they had made the summer before, instead of the No. 32 pick in the second round, they had No. 52. They basically said, "Well, there's no way this kid will be around for us at fifty-two." It didn't seem like I'd land in Toronto.

At the end of workouts, Chad Ford at ESPN ranked me at No. 100 overall. A lot of other places had me going in the late first or no later than the middle of the second round. It was pretty cool, seeing my name on ESPN, and seeing a little NBA.com write-up on me. They asked me all these questions for their blurbs, and I told them, as a joke, that my favourite band was Village People. I was able to enjoy the whole process.

It made things easier that my camp was confident I was going to be drafted.

* * * * *

Chris and Harold decided we should have a viewing party for the draft. We held it at Indian Motorcycle Club in Toronto.

It was a pretty big restaurant, and they set up all these big screens and couches for everyone to watch the draft. Every major news outlet in Canada was there. There were probably twenty cameras. I was a big deal because of the post-Nash excitement and because I'd be playing for the national team. Jamaal Magloire and a few others guys I'd played with stopped by. All of my family flew up for it, too. Aunt Betty was there and was interviewed. Mandy was able to be there beside me, which was great. The day of the draft, my agent took me out to get a suit. It was a big production.

Early in the draft, we were just waiting. I knew I wasn't going to be taken in the lottery, so I was talking to people and signing autographs and being social. Once it got to about twenty in the draft, I focused more. *All right, any time now.* Everyone started watching more closely.

I started getting nervous late in the first round. We were hoping I'd go in the late first or early second, and once my range came around, I was getting butterflies. I started sweating, too, because all of the cameras had bright lights on me during every pick in case they needed to get my reaction. Every time David Stern went to the podium to announce a pick, all the cameras turned back on.

Once the second round started, my phone started blowing up. I was a little confused why teams were calling me. A few of them didn't have any picks left and were trying to get me to commit to Summer League. At first I thought they were calling to tell me they were picking me. I'd answer the phone with, "Yeah, I'll play for anybody, I'm so excited." And they'd say, "No, we have no picks left, we're calling you about Summer League." I'd tell them to call my agent, and they said his phone was off. It was draft night, and my agent's phone was dead. I had

NBA teams calling me instead of him during the draft, and every time I thought that call was going to tell me I got drafted.

I started to feel embarrassed. There were over 100 people there, from media to family and basketball people in the community. This whole time, the cameras were on, so they were capturing my reaction, my disappointment. The draft was into the forties and my phone was blowing up, and every time, they were crushing me. It was an emotional roller coaster.

At a certain point I had to start fighting back tears. I was looking at Chris and Harold like, *What do I do?* My brothers were a pretty rough bunch, and I'm not going to lie, they were ready to take Harold outside. They could see how hurt I was, and their first instinct was to protect me. They were thinking, *Who is this guy? How do you not have your phone on? What the hell are you doing?*

It came around to the Raptors' pick at No. 52, and everyone got excited. Their whole premise had been that I wouldn't be available for them there. I kept popping up on Jay Bilas's list of best players still available on the broadcast. Toronto had traded up for the No. 45 pick a few minutes earlier and taken Matt Bonner, which seemed like a bad sign. For one, it meant they'd added a shooter. It also gave them two rookies already, which might mean a draft-and-stash selection at No. 52.

There had been talk about the Canadian connection. I think they felt pressured. The tough thing for them was if they took me at No. 52 and I wasn't good enough, it would be a PR nightmare to cut me. That was the only logic I could think why they might pass on me. When the Raptors' pick came up, everyone got quiet.

"With the number fifty-two pick in the NBA draft, the Toronto Raptors select Remon van de Hare."

I was heartbroken. Van de Hare was this enormous Dutch kid, seven foot three and 342 pounds. He'd never done much of anything. I understood why teams took international guys, but this was a gut punch. This was the Manu Ginóbili era, when during second-round picks, teams stuffed guys overseas and hoped they would develop, and it wouldn't cost them a thing. That draft had eleven players selected who never ended up playing in the NBA, and most of them were those kind of draft-and-stash guys. Van de Hare never even became a useful player overseas, that's how bad a pick it was.

It was a strange draft. Obviously, it was one of the best drafts ever at the top, and there were some good second-round picks. A lot of guys picked around where I was expected to go ended up being productive NBA guys. Mo Williams was an All-Star, guys like James Jones, Zaza Pachulia, and Keith Bogans had good careers. There were some whiffs, too, and a lot of undrafted players from that year made the NBA.

Korver was taken at No. 51, which should have said something to me. He went on to become an incredible NBA player, but at the time he wasn't any better than me. He shared an agent with Allen Iverson, and those relationships could make the difference on those last picks or roster spots. My agent had no relationships like that. He didn't even have his phone on! All I needed was a chance to get into the right situation, and then I'd know if I was good enough. I didn't have the right people to help me get there.

I wasn't thinking about any of this at the time. I was just trying to keep it together. By the end of the draft, I was sweating more than if I'd played thirty minutes. Every time the draft said a name, the energy went right out of the room. Everyone was feeling bad for me. By the last pick I was thinking, *Please, somebody, just call my name.* They called Andreas Glyniadakis instead, and that was it.

I sat there living a nightmare. I was crushed. This was everything I had ever worked for, this impossible dream that I had made real, coming from a town of seventy, playing on the side of the street. Making it to the NBA was a movie ending.

I thought, *Why did I leave Hawaii? What have I gone and done? Why did I even have a party? That's not me. That's not who I am.* Something small and quiet at my brother's house or a hotel would have suited me a lot more. I'd been excited about getting drafted, so when they suggested it, I just went with it, even though it wasn't me. Now I was sitting there embarrassed.

It was a mix of arrogance and cockiness, disappointment and failure. I was doing everything I could not to cry in front of all of these people and all these cameras.

Once the draft ended, I still had to do interviews for all of the media. It was supposed to be a celebration, and it turned into a wake. Nobody knew what to say to me. I was giving interviews and saying all the right things, things like it would make me stronger and I'd make it to the NBA and prove everybody wrong. Meanwhile, my eyes were red, my face was pale, and Mandy was trying to comfort me and keep me from crying.

I meant those things. My whole life story had been one setback after another, and I'd get back up and fight. But in the moment, this one felt like, *I'm done. This is too much.* This was the ultimate low. I just wanted to get out of there.

My embarrassment wasn't done yet. The suit Harold had bought me was so cheap, and I had been sweating so much, that when I went to get into the car, the entire ass ripped out of my pants. I know it sounds like a bad movie scene, but it happened. The whole ass of my pants ripped out. I had to take my jacket off and wrap it around my waist because my ass was hanging out of my pants, and there were all these cameras, and now everyone could see I was sweating through my shirt. I thought, *Come on, keep it coming.*

Harold was driving me and Mandy to the hotel, and I looked at him and asked, "What the hell just happened? How do you not have your phone? This is a disaster." He tried to console me, and I broke down. I was crying, and I didn't want to talk to anybody. I thought, *Why is this happening to me? Haven't I been through enough already?* After everything that had happened in my life, I'd done everything the right way. I worked hard, I was dedicated, I was a good person. I didn't understand why it wasn't being rewarded.

The next day, all of the headlines read, "English Undrafted." All of these people across Canada had been invested in me, and then they were disappointed. The support was incredible. My neighbour, Jonny McGrath, put up a bunch of white plywood around my net back home so people could come and sign it and show their support. It stretched out for forty-five feet. He had to keep extending it because it became the 2003 version of going viral.

It still hurt. The draft could have been a pinnacle, a defining moment. Outside of my feelings, there was a lot of money on the line, too. As a Canadian athlete with my upbringing, I was a marketable story. I'd had a lot of endorsements lined up that would only kick in if I got drafted. We had deals with Juicy Fruit, General Mills, and General Motors, and those endorsements would have paid me more than my first NBA contract.

Every detail was a train wreck. We met the next day to try to figure things out. It was me, Harold, Chris, and an older gentleman named George Duffield, who had been involved with the process. He was a great man. He was on the outside trying to help steer a bit. He didn't usually speak up too much, but that day he came in really mad. He tore into Chris and Harold, telling them to fix it.

I was sick to my stomach. I understood what it meant to be drafted and what it meant to be trying out. If I were drafted, people were accountable for me as a pick, so they'd give me every chance to succeed. Are they going to keep the guy they invested a pick in, or the guy that came in as a free agent? If ten people had a say in that decision, then ten people's jobs are on the line. It's a business in that way. Undrafted free agents have an uphill battle.

I didn't have much of a choice. I was going to have to play my way into the league.

9

UNDRAFTED. PACERS.

WHEN I WENT UNDRAFTED, it was like starting the pre-draft process all over again.

The draft was in late June, and free agency opened at the start of July, so teams started to get a better picture of what their rosters would look like and how many openings they might have for tryout players. As part of their search, teams would hold free agent mini-camps where undrafted players and veteran free agents or players from overseas would come and try to make an impression.

I managed to get two of those mini-camps lined up right away with two teams who had liked me before the draft: Minnesota and Indiana.

In my draft workout with the Timberwolves, I'd caught their attention because of a shooting drill. The drill was designed to wear you down and see what it took for you to quit. You run end to end in a full sprint taking threes from different spots on the court. Every team had some variation of the drill that they would use late in a workout. Minnesota's worked on a plus-minus system, where if you got to minus eighteen, you were done. The goal was to go as long as you could without reaching minus eighteen. Fatigue was going to win eventually, when a player sprinted back and forth, shooting at the very end of a workout.

One of my biggest assets was always my conditioning. I could run forever, and the draft prep had me in the best shape of my life. I started the drill cold, so almost right away I was at minus fifteen. One more miss and I was done. I was way down in the hole but kept digging my way out. The drill went on for a long time, because I just kept going and was hitting enough shots to get by.

Kevin McHale was their general manager at the time, and he came over afterwards. He said, "I told somebody there that I knew your background and we might be here all day, because that guy's not going to quit. Way to pull yourself out of it. That probably means more than anything else." Minnesota had picked a local kid who never made the team, Rick Rickert, with the No. 55 pick, but they called and were interested in getting me in for another workout.

The other team that was really after me was Indiana. There were rumours before the draft that their pick at No. 49 might be my floor, because everyone knew they liked me. Donnie Walsh had apparently been pushing hard for me, but he was away dealing with a family matter the night of the draft and wasn't in the war room, so they ended up selecting James Jones.

I went to Indiana's mini-camp, and it was a great first taste of life in the NBA. There were all these executives watching and taking notes and talking, just like before the draft. It made me a bit nervous, especially with what I had just gone through. I came in with a big chip on my shoulder. I thought, *I'm not loyal to anybody, I'm coming in here and I'm destroying whoever gets in front of me.*

Well, the person who was put in front of me was Ron Artest.

Ron was the type of guy who was playing any time there was a game going on. It didn't matter if it was a bunch of rookies; he was getting in on the game. We were doing four sessions over two days, and Ron was mixed in.

I was playing well, so they put Ron on me to see how I'd do against an elite defender. He started trash-talking me a little bit, and I thought, *Okay, this is Ron Artest, I can't really say anything.* And that dude was strong as hell. He'd throw me to the ground, and I'd hop back up or hit him with a step-back the next time down. They were impressed with how I handled Ron and was able to stay in rhythm and hold my own. Ron was great, too, chatting me up and giving me some tips.

After the camp was over, Donnie Walsh verbally offered me a contract. He said I was his draft pick. This was on a Friday, and I was supposed to head right to Minnesota for a camp with them on the weekend. I said, "No offence, Donnie. I just got screwed in the draft. I'm going to Minnesota, and I'm not taking a commitment from anyone until it's in writing."

By Tuesday, we had an offer. It was a two-year deal with partial guarantees in each season. Harold leaked to the media that it was fully guaranteed, which it wasn't, but even getting some guarantee to come in and fight for a spot was a great deal for an undrafted player. The partial guarantees were the most money I'd ever seen in my life. I was moving to Indiana.

* * * * *

Before I moved, I had some important business to take care of back home in Newfoundland. I had a plan.

Mandy and I were driving down to Bay Roberts for a family dinner. We left a little early and stopped on the beach at Gooseberry Cove. It's a pretty spot. There's a provincial park there with trails. The ocean gets bright blue in the summer, and the cover curves in to create this small piece of quiet, secluded beach.

We got out of the car, and I blindfolded Mandy. We walked down to the beach, and I told her, "Just trust me. I have a surprise for you."

While she was blindfolded, I wrote, "Will you marry me?" in the sand on the beach. I told her to turn around and take off the blindfold, and when she did, I was down on one knee.

I think it caught her off-guard. There had been so much going on with the draft and trying to make the NBA that the timing surprised her. There was never any doubt we were going to be together—it was just a matter of when. We'd been together since we were kids. She loved me when I was nobody, and I wouldn't have made it through half of what I went through without her. It was important to me that she know how much I loved her and cared about her and appreciated her before we took this next step.

Luckily, she said yes. It was a very, very special day.

We still had to figure out logistics. Mandy was going to come with me to Indiana, which was exciting because, other than during the summer, we hadn't lived in the same place for a few years now. She'd finished her degree in Newfoundland and was considering doing a second one. The Pacers helped her get set up with Indiana University—Purdue University Indianapolis (IUPUI) and put us up in a place in Indianapolis. After all of the heartbreak of the draft, it finally felt like things were coming together.

All I had to do was make the team.

* * * * *

Summer League back in 2003 wasn't the production it is now. There wasn't one major tournament with all thirty NBA teams and every executive and scout in one place. They were smaller and more scattered. It was a lot more about teams evaluating their own guys than a scouting event for the entire league.

That summer, Indiana and Philadelphia split a team in Denver, so my first real action with the Pacers came on a split-squad roster that was half Philadelphia 76ers. The two coaching staffs rotated game by game, so if it was an Indiana game, we'd play more, and if it was a Philadelphia game, their guys would play more. I was back splitting time with Korver.

Donnie Walsh and Larry Bird flew in for our last two games. Larry had just been named president of basketball operations, and those two were the key decision makers. I scored twenty-seven points in the first game they were there. I hadn't played a lot up to that point but found a groove in that one.

That helped set the tone for the summer. I didn't get an off-season as a rookie. It was chaotic with workouts and tryouts, then Summer League, and involuntary workouts that weren't really involuntary when you were trying to make the team. It was important to me that I take advantage of every step, and Summer League was a good start. I came in early for camp to train because I wanted to get right at trying to solidify my spot. A partial guarantee didn't mean you got a spot. I was on the team, but I still had to make the team.

The summer workouts in Indiana were incredible. The organization was full of legendary players and executives. Isiah Thomas was the coach, Chuck Person was in the organization, Larry and Donnie were there, and then I was practising with Reggie Miller some days.

I had a good connection with Coach Thomas. He saw me as more of a combo guard than a point guard and was trying to get me to play that way. After workouts, he'd pull me down to one end of the floor and work with me one on one.

They fired him late in the summer and brought in Rick Carlisle.

Coach Carlisle was a very good coach, but it wasn't the best thing for me as an individual to go from a coach that already liked me to a fresh slate. Coach Carlisle brought in Kenny Anderson late in the off-season for guard depth. Kenny was thirty-three at the time and still a solid point guard, so that was another player to compete with, and as a vet he had Coach Carlisle's trust.

The Pacers had also just re-signed Jermaine O'Neal to a monster seven-year contract, which pushed the team into the luxury tax. When a team was in the luxury tax, every dollar mattered, because every dollar you went over the tax, you'd pay extra to the league. With my contract being only partially guaranteed, it became a situation where cutting me could save them a lot of money compared to cutting someone with a full guarantee.

That someone was Jamison Brewer. He was another young guard. They'd taken him two years before in the second round and he hadn't done much, but he had a guaranteed deal. Once the team signed Kenny, it looked like it would be down to me or Jamison for the final guard spot. That was in my head when camp started. It motivated me. I knew who I had to beat out for a spot, and I knew I had to convince them to keep me, even if it was more expensive.

Training camp was going great. It was a fun experience as a rookie, because I was working my tail off and I was also getting initiated by the vets, which lightened up the atmosphere. We had to pick up doughnuts for the older guys on the team for practices—all the normal rookie duties. We had a fan appreciation event, and all of us rookies had to sing. At first we were trying to fight it. Fred Jones and I didn't want to sing in front of everyone. I'm a bad singer. Reggie threatened to fine us if we didn't sing, so up we went. A few guys on the team had birthdays that month, so we had to sing Happy Birthday, and then we sang, "Go shawty, it's your birthday," from the popular 50 Cent song. James Jones stole the show. He's a terrific singer. The fans had a really good time with it.

I learned a lot having Reggie as a vet. When I first arrived in Indiana, I introduced myself, and he told me, "I know more about you than you know." His girlfriend at the time was from Hawaii, and he used to watch a lot of our games. That was a helpful icebreaker that made me more comfortable working with him right away.

We'd do our normal practices, and then we, the shooting specialists, would go off and do a separate workout. It would be me, James, sometimes Fred, and then Reggie. I was doing these shooting drills, and Reggie Miller was beside me, Chuck "The Rifleman" Person was rebounding for me, Larry Bird was watching me. I was in the presence of some of the greatest shooters and players ever. It was amazing.

Reggie's energy was infectious. He was in his late thirties and had more energy than all of us. He'd make a shot in practice and would scream, "I love this game!" Some of the shots he'd make in a game, I would think, *How did he make that?* And the answer was, well, he practised those. He'd do all these crazy shots after our regular shooting sessions. There were drills where we'd take shots in the toughest situations, and we'd practise them every day so that, if the time came, it wasn't a fluke.

Ron Artest was great, too. He remembered me from the summer mini-camp, and we ended up spending a lot of our recovery time together. We'd play some one-on-one, or we'd do our treadmill work in the pool, and he'd give me little pieces of advice. Once, when I was sitting on the sideline, he came over to me and said, "Stand up. I can sit on the side. Reggie can sit on the side. But you can't ever show these people weakness. Let them know you're always ready."

I appreciated those little things. Ron and I always had a good relationship. He even kicked around the idea of coming to play for St. John's many years later. The guy always wanted to be playing.

My favourite moment of camp might have been the bet I won with Jermaine O'Neal. Jermaine didn't believe I could dunk. I was a white guy, and still kind of skinny at that time, but I was six foot five and really athletic. I said, "Are you serious?" He bet me I couldn't do a dunk. It was a windmill or a 360—whatever the dunk was, I did it, and he had to pay me. He couldn't believe I could dunk.

I didn't play consistently in our pre-season games. Coach Carlisle was trying to get a look at a lot of different guys. I had a good game and scored in double figures in Chicago. There was another game where I sat the entire time, and then with about seventy seconds left, Coach Carlisle put me in. He drew up a play and told me, "I want to see if you can hit a three when it matters and we need it."

I was kind of arrogant at the time. I went out and hit the three, and then we came up with a steal, and I hit another one. I ran by him on the sideline, looked at him, and said, "Is that enough?" I wanted to let him know I was confident enough to hit shots.

This whole time, Jamison wasn't playing. We would talk, and he was pretty sure I was ahead of him. His agent thought he might get traded to Atlanta. Jamison wasn't even practising. He'd go to check into practice, and they'd tell him to sit down because they were trying to move him.

Everything was going well, and then the last four or five days, suddenly they were using Jamison a lot. I was worried. I thought, *Where is this coming from?* He told me, "No, they're keeping you and getting rid of me," and then he would play a bunch. It didn't add up.

I went home to Mandy, and she knew something was wrong. I was wearing it. I had a bad feeling. It seemed like they couldn't move Jamison, and so it was going to come down to dollars and cents, which would be bad news for me. I'd already signed Upper Deck cards, and all of those endorsements I'd lost at the draft were coming back, and all of those things were contingent on me making the team. I tried not to be negative, but I thought, *Here we go again.*

I kept my head down and kept working. I remember the day the cuts were made, I was shooting with Larry for forty-five minutes after practice. He gave me advice on how he got certain shots off, where he'd pump-fake or ball-fake, and how he created space for himself. When we finished, he called me into Coach Carlisle's office.

I was nervous. I was sure I knew what was coming. Larry and Coach Carlisle told me, "We've gotta let you go." Jamison barely played that year. The Pacers didn't play their depth players much because they were a sixty-win team, and so they chose to save on luxury tax with those spots.

I felt like I had failed again. I thought I'd had a strong camp and had done enough to make that team, yet it wasn't good enough. It was a numbers thing, but in the moment it was hard to look at it as being in the wrong situation at the wrong time. Looking at it now, I see all of that and I understand. But in the moment, I looked at it as if I had failed. I left the locker room without even telling the guys.

Telling Mandy was the hardest part, even though I knew she'd be supportive. I had to go home and tell my fiancée, who had moved out there for school to be with me instead of taking offers across Canada, that I wouldn't be living in Indiana anymore. I didn't know where I'd be living. We had an apartment, we had furniture, we had even gotten a dog. I sat her down and broke the news. We both cried. Telling the person I loved, the person I'd just proposed to and moved to start a life with, that our plans had changed, was heartbreaking. I felt like I had failed not just myself but her, too.

I was devastated and embarrassed. Everything had turned upside down again.

10

ROLLER COASTER. D LEAGUE.

THE G LEAGUE IN 2003 wasn't like it is today. Teams didn't own and operate their own affiliates, there were no two-way contracts, and the league was still in the process of figuring out what it wanted itself to be. The National Basketball Development League, as it was known then, had only existed for two seasons, and only seventeen players had ever earned an NBA call-up. It was still an unknown.

The decision to go there after being cut by Indiana was a tough one. My focus had solely been on making the NBA for long enough that I thought it was worth the risk. I had given myself a five-year window where I'd try to make the NBA. I could make more money on overseas offers that were coming in, but it would be easier for NBA teams to see me if I was in the NBDL, and I had my partial guarantee from the Pacers to help make up for some of the salary I'd lose. I'd be a call away if a team needed a shooter on a ten-day contract.

I put my name in for the NBDL and was selected eleventh overall by the Charleston Lowgators.

If you think becoming a Lowgator sounds weird, the other teams in the league at the time were the Altitude, the Riverdragons, the Flight, the Patriots, and the Dazzle. The NBDL was the wild west. It was as strange as the teams' names. Mandy moved to Alberta to work on her occupational degree, her first taste of following me and getting uprooted, while I bused around some of the worst gyms and practice facilities one can imagine.

It was still so new and low-budget that we'd run into problems that professionals shouldn't experience. Once, we were stuck on a twenty-eight-hour bus trip. We practised on concrete at an army base because it was the only court available, and we'd leave with our hands and shoes filthy. We were all making $24,000 or less, so there were no luxuries on the road. It was a grind.

We had a pretty good team in Charleston. Damone Brown had NBA experience, Tierre Brown and Hiram Fuller got call-ups during the year, and Ime Udoka went on to have a solid NBA career and later became a coach. Ime and I became close that year. The grind of minor-league ball bound guys together, even though we were all competing with each other for NBA chances. It was a situation where I'd be disappointed when it wasn't me who got the call, but I'd be happy for my teammates.

I ran into the same issue I had at Hawaii, where the coach, Doug Marty, had his guys whom he trusted and I had to fight for minutes. Ime, Damone, Tierre, and Alpha Bangura had all been there the season before, and Coach Marty trusted Bangura, so he was ahead of me on the depth chart. I'd outplay him in practices and had some good games, and I was playing every day, but I only averaged nineteen minutes.

Not playing a major role hurts in a lot of ways. As a player, I had to try not to press. The more I played, the more chances I had to show people how good I was. That also meant becoming more comfortable and getting more experience. I could play my game and not rush anything. If I was playing less, every minute was such a big opportunity that sometimes I tried to do too much. I didn't let the game come to me as well, and I changed my approach to try to make more of an impact instead of just playing my game. My percentages weren't great that year, I think because I forced it at times, trying to do too much in my minutes.

Playing fewer minutes also hurt my chances for a call-up. Teams that were looking for prospects looked at numbers first, and playing fewer minutes meant my numbers weren't as strong. There was also a perception factor. It never looked good not to be playing a lot. In my case, because I'd been cut by the Pacers and then was a bench player with Charleston, I was worried that it would affect my stock and that teams would think I couldn't hold my own. They'd say, "Well, if he's not even going to play on an NBDL team, how's he gonna make it up here?" I was playing less and making it worse by pressing.

A couple of the other teams in the league wanted me for a bigger role, and we tried to get Charleston to trade me. It wasn't personal. I was stuck behind Bangura, who wasn't an NBA player by any means, and other teams would use me in a more prominent role. Charleston wouldn't trade me because they knew other guys might get called up, and they'd need depth for the playoffs. We lost in the first round.

I felt like I was right back where I started heading into the off-season, trying to make an impression from scratch.

* * * * *

The summer was a lot like when I went undrafted: a lot of mini-camps and workouts for teams, as well as my first time with the senior men's national team for Canada. I had changed agents late in the season after I couldn't get traded from Charleston, so I felt I had a fresh start heading into the 2004–05 season. I was trying to put last year behind me.

It felt like things were going the right way when the Seattle Super-Sonics called. They didn't offer any guaranteed money, but they did offer a chance to come into training camp and compete, which was enough for me.

I'd been fortunate to spend my first NBA camp with Reggie Miller and Larry Bird, and I got to spend my second with Ray Allen. For a shooting specialist, there wasn't much better learning on the job than to practise and work out with those guys. Watching how someone like Ray prepared and approached his craft stuck with me. I always tried to pick up little things from established guys that I could add to my own game or routine.

Ray, Luke Ridnour, and I used to play a shooting game where the losers had to call the winner "King" for the day. I won a couple of times. Not many times, but a couple. You're not going to beat Ray Allen too often. I had a good camp. Head Coach Nate McMillan ran intense practices, and between those and working with Ray, I learned a lot. They needed a shooting guard, and I was competing for that spot.

They'd also signed Ibo Kutluay to a two-year deal that summer, so I was in an uphill battle. Kutluay was thirty and coming off some strong years in Greece and Turkey, and teams trying to win right away, like Seattle, would usually favour someone with more experience, especially if they'd invested in them. The mistake I made was trying to change my game once they brought in Kutluay. I thought because he filled their need for a shooting guard that I had to become more of a point guard. If one spot was filled, I'd fight for another.

I tried to be a player that I wasn't, which I thought was the right thing to do at the time. When Coach McMillan sat me down to tell me I'd been cut, he told me, "Do what got you here. You changed your game to be a point guard when you're a combo guard and a scorer. That's what got you to this point. Don't change for me or for anybody. Be what you are and go wherever that takes you." That stuck with me for the rest of my career. I know that my intentions were in the right place trying to make the team, but he was right.

Ray was great when they let me go. He pulled me aside and told me, "You've proven to them and to yourself that you deserve to be here. Don't let it get you down. They have to give this other guy a chance, but you proved you're good enough."

I thought I'd gotten really close again. I was disappointed and frustrated but thought I just needed to catch a break. Now I needed a real chance, and the best place to get that chance was in the NBDL. I still had money from the Pacers, so I decided to give the NBDL one more try.

* * * * *

Charleston had become the Florida Flame that off-season and still held my rights. The conditions had improved a lot, which made the season more tolerable. There were better practice facilities and housing, and the people who'd invested to move the team seemed motivated.

They'd also made Dennis Johnson the coach. He was terrific. He had so many stories to tell about his time in the league, and because most of the veterans from the year before weren't back, he wanted to play me in a primary role. I played nearly thirty minutes a game and shot the heck out of the ball, hitting 45.7 per cent of my threes.

There was a catch with my three-point shooting, though. Another bump in my road.

The NBA has always used the NBDL as a place to experiment, and that year they were experimenting with an awful rule change. The league's three-point explosion hadn't occurred yet, but for some reason the league wanted to cut down on threes, or make them rarer and more exciting. For the 2004–05 season, three-pointers only counted in the final three minutes of each quarter in the NBDL.

The experiment was a big failure for the league. The games slowed down because there was more attacking, less space, and way more free throws, and teams would just play zone until three-pointers were allowed.

For a player like me, that rule change was a disaster. Because I was a starter, a lot of my minutes came when threes didn't count. I'd play the first few minutes of each half, come out before the quarter was over, then play most of the second and fourth quarters. Maybe six minutes out of my thirty each game were played when threes counted.

Coach Johnson didn't want me to change my game and told me to shoot long twos if they were open to me. Coaches only got a few weeks' notice about the change, so it wasn't like he had time to overhaul his offence, anyway. The encouragement was nice, but it still didn't help those long twos count as threes.

I was a three-point specialist, and NBA teams looking at my stats would notice the percentages, but I'd hardly taken any attempts. I went twenty-one for forty-six in forty-eight games. I took a lot of shots from behind the three-point line when they counted as twos, but they didn't keep those stats specifically, so a team might not know how well I was shooting. Since I was known as a shooter, NBA teams were looking at me for a specialist role, and I didn't have the numbers to support that. It also hurt my overall scoring. I averaged 14.6 points, and that could have been higher if my threes had actually counted as threes.

I tried to stay hopeful I'd get a call-up because my percentages were so good. If a team needed a shooter, they'd look and see the percentages, they'd ask around, and Coach Johnson would tell them what I was doing. I'd still get frustrated it was hurting my chances.

It didn't help that Matt Carroll shot over sixty per cent on his threes that year, too. We'd have games going back and forth trading threes, and he was just ahead of me on the leaderboard. If a team needed a shooter, it was going to be him or me. He eventually got called up and stayed in the NBA for a decade.

I changed agents again midway through that season, because my new agent wasn't returning my calls once I got cut by Seattle. Chris helped me set up interviews with a few different agents, and I ended up with Justin Zanik. Justin is the general manager of the Utah Jazz now, so, needless to say, he was pretty good at his job. I finally had a capable agent, which helped turn things around.

The Orlando Magic called Justin in March and told him they wanted to bring me in.

The NBDL season was almost over, and that late in the NBA season, a ten-day contract could easily turn into a rest-of-season contract. Even if I didn't play much, it was an opportunity to get in with a team before the summer and show them what I could do and who I was as a person and a teammate. It could be a head start on a tryout for the next year, which to me was more valuable than a little bit of extra cash.

We agreed to sign a ten-day. John Weisbrod, the general manager, called me and told me to pack my stuff and that the team was excited to bring me in. The Magic were practising that night, and he had me rush to the airport so that I would be available for their shootaround and game the next day. I had two or three hours to get all my gear together, clear out my locker, and get on a 1:00 a.m. flight.

This was it. I'd gotten my call. All of the pain and hard work of the last two years was about to pay off, and once they let me in the door, I was going to make sure they kept me.

I was already at the airport when John called again. He said, "We can't sign you. Hedo Türkoğlu's wrist is broken. We can't bring you in now, but we're gonna follow you." They needed another forward instead of a guard to fill Türkoğlu's spot. They signed Mark Jones instead.

All I could think was, *You've gotta be kidding me.*

I had my ticket. I was at the airport. All I had to do was fly there and sign the contract. My NBA dream had come true. And it had all been taken away again. I was starting to become numb to the disappointment.

Justin had kept me informed of the interest in me overseas. After the Magic deal fell through, I called him and told him, "Man, I'm done with this roller coaster."

11

WORLD TRAVELLER. OVERSEAS.

WITH THE WAY THE LAST two years had gone, trying to crack the NBA, I was ready to try something new.

Even with the partial guarantee from the Pacers, taking NBDL salaries over much larger overseas contracts was something I could only do for so long, especially with the frustration that had built up with how many close calls I'd had. I was ready to start a new chapter and try to find a different way back to the NBA. That meant trying to establish myself overseas.

There was something pretty big to take care of first. On August 5, Mandy and I got married.

It was something I knew I'd wanted to do since I was a kid. We got married in St. Bride's, Newfoundland, where Mandy grew up and just around the way from where I grew up. It felt right to do it at home rather than in the city or wherever my career took us next. Small-town Newfoundland was a big part of both of us and where we'd met and grown as partners.

We'd been together as long as I could remember, and I knew that whatever was going to come next, I wanted to do it with her.

We'd been apart the last two seasons and were going to be apart again the coming year while she finished her occupational therapy program at the University of Alberta. There were no worries about the distance because we'd done it so long between Hawaii and my two NBDL years. Sometimes people struggle with long-distance relationships, but it worked for us. It gave her time to focus on her degrees and allowed me to focus solely on basketball day to day. When things got difficult, she was always there as my rock.

It's hard to capture just how important Mandy was to me through the tragedies and the disappointments I'd dealt with. The cliché that behind every good man there's a great woman is a cliché for a reason. With Mandy, it was an understatement. She was the one person I always knew had my back.

As I got older, I learned that not everyone supports you for the right reasons and that I had some naïveté from growing up in a small Newfoundland community where everyone trusted everyone. I'd broken off ties with Chris that same summer once I started realizing that. The signs were there, and I finally noticed them. It all drove home that I had to know whom I could trust and keep the right people around me. Mandy had been my best friend since I was young, my best friend through everything, and she loved me when I was nobody.

My career was about to take me all over the world, and I was incredibly lucky Mandy was coming along for the ride.

* * * * *

Before I went overseas, I gave Summer League another try. Justin and I were considering a lot of overseas offers, and there was nothing guaranteed being offered in the NBA, so it was about keeping my name and face out there and seeing if something might click.

Nothing did. I went to Las Vegas with the Cleveland Cavaliers and played a few minutes over five games. They'd used a first-round pick on Luke Jackson the year before, and he took most of the minutes as the shooting specialist, and bench minutes were spread thin because there were seventeen players on the roster.

That's how Summer League went sometimes. It was similar to going into camp as an undrafted player instead of as a draft pick. People had their guys they'd invested in or argued for, and those guys were going to get the first opportunities. Some of the roster spots were given out as favours to friends or family of a team's star players, or to an agent's other clients. I learned to deal with it. I was frustrated enough with trying to make the NBA that it didn't affect me as much anymore.

After my wedding, I went to the Dominican Republic with the national team for the 2005 FIBA Americas Championship. I'd played for the under-twenty-one team back in 2000 and performed exhibitions with them the summer before, but this was my first official FIBA event with the senior team.

Right away, I saw what made playing for the national team so special. I was hooked.

This was at a point in Canadian basketball when we struggled a lot to accomplish anything at the international level. Many of our goals were based on doing well enough to qualify for the next event rather than medalling. We were realistic about our talent level, that our program was behind some of the other Americas teams. The plan was to build and gain experience, and then attract more of our top guys if we could qualify for a World Cup or an Olympics. The Olympics was always the big goal. They'd made it in 2000, and everyone raved about that experience.

Steve Nash wasn't playing with the team any longer, and we had no other NBA players, so the tournament was a tough one. The US didn't send any of their NBA guys down, either, and we beat them early on. We lost the rest of our games, finishing 1-3 and failing to advance.

It was a great experience for me. I led the team in scoring with eighteen points per game, which was top ten in the tournament, and I hit more than half of my threes. It wasn't the result I'd been hoping for, but the learning experience of being our top option against teams like Brazil and Venezuela was invaluable.

I also think I opened some eyes and built some momentum heading to Italy.

* * * * *

I'd decided to sign with Virtus Bologna of the Italian Lega A, which was the top division in Italy.

Virtus had a storied history and had won two EuroLeague championships in the few years before, including one in 2001 with Manu Ginóbili before he went to the NBA. They'd had a lot of trouble since then—they went bankrupt and were dropped to the second division for a couple of seasons. This would be their first year back in Lega A after finding a new owner, so they were trying to load up to regain their earlier prestige.

That made an interesting opportunity for me. They were a club with a great reputation, a new owner, a big budget, and they needed guys. They'd hired Zare Markovski as head coach, and he really liked me and pushed for me to come.

The decision wasn't easy. I was frustrated with the NBA, but it was still my dream. I'd used each disappointment to push me to work even harder to achieve that dream. If I went to Europe, there was no chance of an in-season call-up, and there was a risk that if I didn't play well or didn't put up big numbers, I might not be noticed.

The offer Virtus made would set me up financially for a while, and so I thought that if nothing else it would give me some cushion if I wanted to try the NBA again after the season. That whole year, my focus remained on the NBA. Many Americans had gone overseas and made it back, and I thought this would be a good chance to make some money, see the world, and improve my stock for the next season. If I went to Virtus and killed it, none of those other factors would matter.

It was a big adjustment to make. It was a culture shock, and the language barrier was tough. I didn't speak Italian, and Bologna wasn't a city where you could speak much English. Mandy was finishing up in Alberta, so I was living on my own, and I was unable to communicate properly.

In the first two weeks I was there, I was fined 3,000 euros because I kept driving in the bus lanes. It was the shortest route to practice, and I couldn't read any of the signs. When I'd get pulled over, the police didn't speak English. Nobody took pity. Nobody cared. They just charged my account, and on they went.

European contracts included things like a car, house, insurance, even a TV and Internet. I learned the lesson pretty quickly that if I didn't explicitly get something written in my contract, I wasn't going to get it. If I wanted a long-distance plan, I had better get my agent to put that in the contract. If I wanted a dryer so I didn't have to hang my practice clothes on a drying rack every day, I'd better get that in the contract—I was responsible for washing my own gear.

There was a basketball adjustment, too. The culture around the sport was a little different. In the NBA, every aspect was the best of the best, whereas in Europe they might not have the same level of facilities, travel, equipment, or even post-game meals. Whatever they put out was what we got to eat, and we couldn't leave a meal until the coach dismissed us with our instructions. On some teams and with some coaches, it was very military-like. Some North Americans went over and struggled with that structure and with not being as coddled.

I'd gotten pretty used to the NBDL grind, so moving to a good club in Italy was a step up. But I also remembered what things were like with the Pacers and Sonics. Playing in Europe was somewhere in between the two. If the NBA sent their rookies to play internationally for a year, I thought it would extend their time in the NBA. It was an eye-opener about what other leagues were like and how good guys in the NBA had it, and it would make you want to work even harder to get back there and stay there.

Luckily, I had some good teammates to help with the adjustment. David Blutenthal and Ken Lacey were a pair of Americans on the team, and there was Marko Milič, who was the first Slovenian in the NBA and was well-known for winning a couple of Dunk Contests overseas. They helped out with the things I hadn't thought of when I headed over there, like how to set up my banking and how to transfer money.

We would get bonuses for our wins, 1,500 or 2,000 euros per win, and we won nineteen games that year. I spent a little bit of it and had a bunch left over. I didn't know how to get it home. There were limits on how much cash you could bring across the border. The guys told me what they'd done in the past, like putting it in their tights or cutting pages out of books in which to hide it, or concealing the money under the soles of their shoes.

David and Ken helped me figure a lot of that out, and then I would pass it on to guys in future seasons. The imports on a team always tended to bond together, because there were usually only a couple on a roster, and those were the players you could communicate with and with whom you had similar experiences. We tried to have everyone together, but those groups form naturally.

The FIBA game was different than the NBA. The coaching styles were different, and with so many imported players on one-year contracts, there was always a lot of uncertainty about my future, my role, and how invested a team was in me. If I came in as a Canadian or an American, there was a bit of a Catch-22: slots for imported players were limited, so we had a great deal of pressure to perform or get cut. Also, coaches didn't trust us as much initially, especially when we were new to the international game. It was like being a rookie again, even though I'd played two seasons professionally and nearly made the NBA a couple of times.

That's changed a lot over the years. Basketball has gone global enough to knock down some of those barriers. It used to be that Italy thought it had the best league, Spain thought it had the best league, Croatia . . . and so on, and everyone thought the way they ran their leagues and approached basketball was the best way. Now it's more accepted that the NBA sets the pinnacle, then the big EuroLeague clubs that could compete with NBA teams, and then on down from there. Decision makers understand that now, which is why I think you see more free movement between the NBA and the top European leagues.

At the time, that wasn't the case. It even extended to the officiating. In the first pre-season tournament I played in, I scored over twenty points in a game but was called for eight or nine travels. FIBA had some different rules, but a travel was a travel. I was a new import, so I wasn't going to get any benefit of the doubt.

Coach Markovski was a great coach, but he was strict. He did things his way. I remember one time he looked at me and said I'd run the floor in seven or eight steps, and he thought I could do it in five or six. He would count my steps as I ran the court. He'd make us practise these different hops, European hops similar to how the Euro step has become popular in the NBA. I thought, *Am I ever going to use any of this in a game?*

We'd practise twice a day, sometimes three times ahead of a big game. We'd play on Saturday, take Sunday off, and then get right back to two-a-days. Practices there were much more intense than in the NBA, too. We might only play once a week, so we could go harder in practice than the NBA could with eighty-two games, and the coaches wanted everything to be perfect before a game. If I was hurt and couldn't practise, I couldn't play. There was no taking it easy during the week and then hopping into a game. It took a toll.

I played pretty well once the season got going. I hit forty per cent of my threes, which was always a good benchmark to reach if teams were looking for shooters. My numbers were modest because my role would change game to game. I started sixteen games, came off the bench for nine, sometimes played big minutes, sometimes small minutes.

I struggled to understand what Coach Markovski wanted. The language barrier was a factor, even with a translator for the English-speaking players. I had my best game of the year, but one of my teammates got back-doored on the last play of the game and we lost. Coach thought it was my fault for not pressuring the ball well enough, even though it wasn't me who lost his man. He was losing his mind in the locker room, yelling at me, "What do you think this is? This is not basketball. What you learned is not basketball."

In the practice after that game, I tried to make up for it. I wanted to prove him wrong, so I went at it hard and took it seriously. He got upset and stopped practice. He asked me what was wrong, and I said I wanted to do better and I wanted to win. Coach sent us all home. He said, "Carl won't smile, we'll go home." Another time, I'd struggled in a game and went out after the game to get some shots up. That was a normal thing players do, especially at home. I went and shot on our rims to try to get some feel and rhythm back. The organization didn't like that, and Coach Markovski deactivated me for the next game.

The fans there liked me, so while I was on the bench that game, they sang my song. Every player there had a song the fans would sing to support them, and the fans sang mine even though I was inactive. I was sent home at halftime of that game for being a distraction. I was just sitting there! I appreciated it, but I hadn't done anything. After a few games, Coach activated me and put me in the starting lineup for our big city rivalry game with Fortitudo Bologna. I played well, only to be deactivated the next game.

It was up and down like that all year. The strangest part was that I thought Coach Markovski didn't like me because he'd been so hard on me, but after the season I was told that he was talking me up to other teams and strongly recommending me when other clubs asked about me. I thought he hated me, and here he was helping me land my next contract!

I was only on a one-year deal, and between my shooting and the coach vouching for me, I had some options that summer.

* * * * *

That whole first season in Italy, I was thinking of how close I'd been to the NBA, first with the Pacers and then with the Magic call-up. It was hard not to think like that. I was away from home and away from Mandy again, and I wanted so badly for these sacrifices to pay off. When I was by myself, I had a lot of time for my mind to run and go through those what-ifs.

I put all of that aside and didn't even go the mini-camp or Summer League route in 2006. Mandy was finished school and was going to come with me wherever I went next, and that made the idea of another season overseas more attractive.

One of the teams Coach Markovski had recommended me to was Zadar in the Croatian ABA League. His mother was from Zadar, and he had a house there, so he had some connections with the team. They were coming off a good league year in which they had won the Croatian Cup, but they'd been knocked out of EuroCup, which was the third-tier European competition at the time. Like Virtus the year before, they were looking to make a push back up the ladder, and I was a part of their plan.

Croatia is rich in basketball history. Justin gave me a bit of a history lesson when he was selling me on it. He also laid out the hard truth of where I was in my career. He said, "The money is still good. About the same as Virtus. But now you need to have a good year. You're coming off a subpar year your first year—now you have to go and dominate to get back to where you want to be." It was a matter of getting somewhere that I could show who I really was. Zadar fit.

It was foreign to me initially. I tried to research online what it would be like, and I remember thinking, *Where the heck are we going?* Having Mandy with me helped with the adjustment. Having someone there for me at the end of the day was a welcome change. We had a nice little condo right along the Adriatic Sea, and the food there was fabulous, so the set-up outside of basketball was great. It's still one of my favourite places I've played.

The support from the fans in the city was incredible. Croatia was such a mecca for basketball, and the fans cared about everything. They would watch and critique players' fundamentals—practices were open to the public—and every fan had an opinion on the team and the game and the style of play. The noise at games was crazy, too. Someone would score and the place would go up, and you would see all of these puffs of smoke because fans were smoking in the gym. At halftime of one of my first games there, I went up the stairs from our locker room and I couldn't see the far hoop because there was so much smoke in the gym.

Playing road games in Croatia was an adventure. Every time we flew into these cities, we would have police cars in front and behind, just to be safe. We were on the road in Šibenik once, and they put us in an armoured bus. I thought, *What the heck is going on?* The year before, a visiting bus had been stoned by Šibenik fans and a few players got hurt, so they were doing this as a safety measure. It didn't work. As we warmed up for that game, fans threw flares onto the court. Flares lit up all around, and one almost caught our coach's pants on fire. We all had to go back with security to the locker room while they ejected the fans. For safety, we played that game in an empty gym.

The team was doing well but didn't quite meet the standards of the people in the community, so they fired the coach partway through the season. They hired Aco Petrović, Dražen's brother. I've been coached by some of the greats, but hearing Coach Petrović tell stories about Dražen might be the peak. It was very cool. And then things started turning around, and we started playing really well.

I had a bit of a swagger to me when I got to Croatia, because I had finally let go of the constant NBA chase, and that was freeing, mentally. It wasn't eating me up inside as much anymore. I'd chosen to stay overseas to improve as a player, and for now I'd made peace with not making the NBA. I was on a mission to get better and prove myself, and then I could think about the NBA later.

Everything had quickly fallen into place for me. I got there, and I was dominating as we got ready for the season, and for the first time since Hawaii, that meant I was playing a big role right away. I was on fire. I averaged 21.6 points, 4.2 rebounds, 2.8 assists, and 1.6 steals across the Croatian League and the Adriatic League, and I hit forty per cent of my threes again.

I had missed a big opportunity with scouts halfway through the year. I'd had a couple of big games in a row in December and January, and then I pulled a muscle. I missed three weeks, and during that time a large group of scouts came in. Mike Dunleavy was there with them. It sucked to be sitting on the bench for that one. I was in this little gym full of smoke with 3,800 people jammed in, and there was Mike Dunleavy.

I missed out on that, and I felt I needed to close the year strong to cement my status heading into the summer—if I played.

Going into the first round of the playoffs, the team was having money problems. They were behind on paying me, which was fairly typical in Europe. I'd heard so many horror stories about empty promises and non-payment that I said, "Look, I'm not coming to practice. If you don't pay me, I'm not showing up." I was making a stand. Playing overseas, I had an agent in that country along with my main agent, so my Croatian agent was the one trying to handle all of this. I no-showed a practice, and the next day I said I wasn't getting on the bus to the game. They showed up at my house with cash so I'd get on the bus and play.

We went on to place second in the Croatian League, win the Croatian Cup, and come seventh in the Adriatic League. It was a successful season for Zadar. It was their third Croatian Cup in a row, and they were going to be back up to the ULEB Cup the following season, one tier below EuroLeague.

I enjoyed that year so much because I achieved a high level of success at a high level of basketball. I was an all-star in the Adriatic League and won MVP of the all-star game, all of which helped me build interest. Thanks to the season we had and the numbers I put up, I was getting EuroLeague interest and heavy interest from Euro-Cup teams. I was going to be able to double my money and jump to a higher league.

First, I figured, *Hey, if my season got me this kind of European interest, maybe the NBA will be interested now.* Coming off the best season of my career, I was going to give the NBA another shot.

12

Spanish Rock Star. Overseas II.

IF I WAS GOING TO turn a strong European season into an NBA opportunity, there was no better place than the San Antonio Spurs, the team that built a dynasty with international imports.

The Spurs brought me in for a workout and ran me through what was called the Brent Barry Drill. In between scrimmages, the Spurs had me shoot 100 threes, all on the move and in different situations. There were ten curls, then ten curl-fades, ten transition threes, ten flares, and so on. The record at the time was 92 out of 100.

I went in there after consecutive seasons hitting forty per cent of my threes and shooting well in college and the NBDL before that. That's what I was—a shooter. The drill was tough and pushed my conditioning, but the threes were unguarded, so I quickly got into a rhythm. I started out hot and was hitting threes all over the place. It caught people's attention in the gym because it looked like I might threaten the record.

I came up just short, finishing with 88 or 89. They said to me, "We didn't know you shot like this." I thought, *Well, if you watched me at all, you'd know I'm a shooter*, but I bit my tongue.

The scrimmages didn't go as well. The tough thing with mini-camps was that everyone was trying to make an impression, and everyone was unfamiliar with each other. I wasn't getting many shots. The mistake I made was trying to force shots to make an impression. I was a shooter, and I didn't want to go through games without them seeing I could shoot in a game situation. I opened myself up to mistakes by being impatient and took some shots I shouldn't have.

I think that showed my immaturity at the time. I was trying so hard to show how good I was that I'd try to do everything in ten seconds. If I had gone in there and shot well in drills, and then taken fewer shots as they came to me, that might have made a better impression. Coach Gregg Popovich and the rest of the Spurs staff were smart—the Spurs were always looking for players to fit a role and the system. They probably would have understood me taking fewer shots because of the flow of the game rather than me trying to do too much. My attitude should have been to control what I could control and not worry about how many shots I was getting. It was a good lesson to take forward.

My next stop was Toronto.

I was excited. I thought I'd have a pretty good chance because there would be no pressure on the team this time and because it would make for a good story. There was a little bit of hype about the mini-camp, more than usual. Everyone had watched me with the national team by then and heard about my season in Europe. I was still disappointed how the draft had played out, but I'd established myself since then, and they had gotten a new general manager and a new head coach, so it was a fresh opportunity.

Sam Mitchell was the new coach, and he was a big trash-talker. I walked in for the mini-camp in jeans and flip-flops and said hello to some of the staff and media there. Right away, Coach Mitchell started running his mouth. He said, "I hear you're a shooter. Come shoot." But I was in flip-fops. He told me it didn't matter. So, I went over and beat him in a shooting competition wearing flip-flops. At the end, all he told me was, "You better bring it tomorrow, young fella."

I played well in the camp. Jay Triano was an assistant under Coach Mitchell, and we had a good relationship, which helped. I left camp thinking there was a good chance I would make the team.

The one person standing in my way was Jamario Moon. It came down to the two of us. I thought I had a better camp, but Jamario jumped out of the gym every time he touched the ball. We'd take a water break, and he'd dunk from the free-throw line, catching the attention of all of the executives there. He had a good story, too, as a guy who had been all over the NBDL and some other leagues and hadn't gone to a big college. He was a good defender and could run the floor, but he just wasn't all that skilled.

The Raptors went with Jamario, which worked out for them. He was a fan favourite, he went to the NBA Slam Dunk Contest, and he played seven years in the league.

It was another tough blow for me. I thought I'd had a great camp. I shot well, and everyone liked me. And because it was just a mini-camp, teams didn't have to explain it to me, so I wasn't sure what I'd missed or done wrong. I'd had good years in the NBDL and with Zadar, and I was an all-star and second in a good league in scoring. I started to think it just wasn't going to happen.

Houston liked me and wanted me to come in for Summer League. I was supposed to get there on a Thursday, and I busted my ankle up pretty badly in a workout that Tuesday.

I told them I still wanted to come and could push through it. When I got there, their doctors told me there was no way I could do anything. I explained to them that these chances were rare and that I'd played through ankle injuries before. They relented and let me play.

My ankle was heavily taped up, and I was doing therapy for it before and after practices. But it was showing. I could barely practise. I'd get by a guy and go to push off, and suddenly he'd catch up and cut me off. I had no burst.

They made me slow down for a week with the hope I'd be ready for Summer League. I went with them to Las Vegas and got into one game. I hit a pair of threes quickly, bang-bang, and then never got to play again. I thought I could push through, but I didn't get the chance. I thought, *Man, I'm done with this.*

The coaches told me I'd get more opportunity later in the tournament once a few other guys left, but that wasn't a great consolation. My agent was worried that if I wasn't playing it would hurt my stock. It was poor optics to barely play at Summer League, and you didn't want to publicize that the reason was an injury, because then teams would worry about your injury.

I pulled out of Summer League to focus on the rest of the off-season and let my ankle heal. I'd done enough that NBA teams were interested but not enough to make guaranteed offers. Sometimes teams would throw $25,000 or $100,000 as a guarantee to bring guys into camp to compete, which made it a tougher choice. There was a risk of going into camp and not getting a chance to show enough. If I was fighting for one of those last few spots and then got cut, I'd have the small guarantee, but it would be too late to turn around and get a good deal overseas.

I had bigger money on the table in Europe, more than I would make at the low end of the NBA. This was my fifth summer of trying to make the NBA, and the roller coaster of the last couple of years had taken its toll on me. Every year, I'd gone right from my season into mini-camps and Summer League, played for the national team, then gone right back to camp. Don't get me wrong, I'm not complaining about eleven months of basketball. But there was a mental fatigue that set in, and I was a little fed up with the constant disappointment.

I decided to take an offer in Spain with Gran Canaria instead of fighting for a job at an NBA training camp.

* * * * *

Before I left for Spain, I joined the national team for the 2007 FIBA Americas Championship in Las Vegas.

The tournament was a much bigger deal than it had been in 2005, because the US were sending a full NBA roster. The Americans had only won bronze at the 2004 Olympics, and 2008 was gearing up to be the next version of the Dream Team for them, and they saw 2007 on home soil as a good tune-up. That meant Kobe Bryant, LeBron James, Carmelo Anthony, and a roster full of other NBA All-Stars.

Our team was better, too. I was hitting my prime and was established in the program. Denham Brown was in the same position, and we had some younger players like Levon Kendall and Andy Rautins coming up. Samuel Dalembert was playing, too.

It was a good tournament for us as a program that was still growing. The US beat us by fifty. I didn't hit a shot the entire game, but it was a great experience to play against that level of competition. We finished 4-4 overall and came in fifth, which was a good result for Canada at the time.

That tournament ran into September, and the Spanish season started in early October, so there was only a quick stop home in Newfoundland in between.

Spain itself was beautiful. The team was located in Las Palmas on the Canary Islands, off the coast of Africa, which was an incredible place to live. When I'd researched Croatia online, it left me a little uncertain. That wasn't the case with Canaria. I also liked the idea of hopping to another island and being somewhere near the beach again. The adjustment was easier because I was in my fourth country in four years, I was more open to different cultures, and my wife was with me. I was making more money, too, which helped, since Mandy couldn't work without a special visa.

It was a great move, from a basketball perspective. The Spanish league was the best national league in the world outside of the NBA, and EuroCup was just one tier down from EuroLeague, so the level of competition was going to be high, which would be good for my development and my stock. I was going to play against guys like Marc Gasol, Ricky Rubio, and Rudy Fernández. One of the reasons I'd chosen Gran Canaria over a EuroLeague team in a different country was that Maurizio Gherardini, who was with the Raptors and a major power broker internationally, told me Spain was valued highly by NBA teams from a financial and competitive standpoint.

Our team was strong and had a lot more English-speaking players, which helped in terms of communication. James Augustine, Melvin Sanders, and Jim Moran were on the roster from the US, Joel Freeland from Britain, and we had Sitapha Savané from

Senegal. The big thing everywhere in Europe, especially Spain, was passports. Every national league had a limit on import players, and because Spain produced so many guards itself, they didn't often bring in many guards. The more imports a team could get that had a European passport, the better. That was how the top teams built their rosters.

A lot of guys tried to get passports for those reasons. Many Americans overseas didn't play for the US national team, so one of the easiest ways was to play for a country's basketball federation as a naturalized player. Players would offer to play for a country's national team, they'd get a passport, and then they would have more opportunities in European leagues because they didn't take up one of the import roster spots. That would increase a player's job opportunities and salary.

That wasn't an option for me, because I played for Canada. There were always rumours about guys buying passports, and some guys ended up marrying someone overseas and getting a passport that way. That wasn't exactly an option for me, either. So, I always played on my Canadian passport and counted as an import. That was how we managed to get such a good roster, though—a lot of Americans with overseas passports.

We finished ninth in the ACB that year, missed the playoffs, and did well in the ULEB Cup. I led the team in scoring with over fifteen points per game and hit 38.4 per cent on threes, so it was another big step forward for me, individually. I'd carried over my success from a smaller league to a higher level and was the top option on a good team. That raised my stock in Europe even higher, and even though in my head I was done with the NBA for the time being, it didn't hurt there, either.

It also made me a popular person around the city and a hated man in other cities. Spanish fans were intense about their basketball, so when we were on the road, we were almost always hearing a lot of trash talk. I'd give it back a little bit, as usual, and sometimes that would get me into a bit of trouble.

We were in Seville for a road game that year, and I was having a good night. One of their players was getting into me and getting very physical, and I hit a few shots in a row against him and got right up in his face after a whistle. I got called for a technical, then I started talking to the fans and told them, "Shhh," after making baskets. They taunted right back. We won the game, and I gave it to the fans a little bit more.

I thought it was all in good fun. It was part of the competition and the passion. I went outside after the game, and seven or eight fans were waiting for me. They all surrounded me, and honestly I was scared, because my teammates were already on the bus and I didn't know how serious these fans were. They were ready to fight.

I said, "Hold on, guys. Did you have fun? Was it good entertainment? I loved how you guys were getting on me. I had fun." And they said they had fun, too. One of them spoke up and said, "Next year, English, you play for us and everything is okay." I just wanted to get out of there, so I agreed, and then they were asking for pictures. We all hugged, and I booked it out of there.

I'd play for Seville eventually, just not the next year. Of all the teams I've played for in my international career, Gran Canaria was the only one I'd go back to for a second year.

* * * * *

On November 6, 2008, my son, Ryder, was born.

Playing in a place like Spain, there was a lot of pressure to play through anything. They were paying me a lot of money and they owned my rights, and the culture with European basketball was that you showed up and played every game. There was no, "I'm going to take a day off."

I didn't want to miss the birth of my first child. Part of the reason I chose Gran Canaria was that Mandy and I felt it would be a good place to have the baby. The health care was good, and Mandy was comfortable with the situation. I didn't want to be a continent away when my child was born, and I certainly didn't want to miss his birth if Mandy was nearby.

The team had a EuroCup road game in Turkey, and I told them I wasn't going. Everyone with the team was mad at me. In the back of my mind, I was hoping Mandy would have the baby while they were on the road trip so that I'd be justified in missing the game. If the team came back and the baby wasn't born, they'd say I should have been there. The head nurse who helped deliver Ryder was one of the team's biggest fans. She knew who we were and was excited, and she knew I was missing the game.

Ryder came while the team was on the trip back from Turkey. I'd caught a break. It was a big weight off, as silly as that may sound. And then I was able to rejoin the team for a home game right after.

Mandy's mom came out to help with Ryder for a while. My brother Michael came out, too. That little bit of help went a long way. Mandy was such a soldier through all of it. I would have to go to practice twice a day for two and a half hours, or I would go on road trips with the team, and she was low-key through all of it. When she was pregnant, there wasn't much she could do. But when Ryder arrived, her hands were full. It was just the two of them at the house a lot of the time.

Mandy always allowed me to focus on my job while she took care of things at home. Becoming a father put that into perspective, and it made me realize that I wasn't living just for myself anymore. I was a father now, and I had to make sure that I was a role model. I wanted to be everything to this little guy, as a man and as a provider.

I thought maybe that would put more pressure on me to perform. Instead, it helped me realize that basketball was just a game. It had been my whole life and my sole focus for so long, and I'd made a lot of sacrifices for it. I still loved it, and it was still how I'd provide for my family, but I had to be less selfish about the decisions I made around basketball. We were in a foreign country with a new baby and our families a long flight away, so I couldn't move around on a whim if an opportunity came up.

With every decision I had to consider the impact on my family. With any city I considered, we had to look at the availability of English-speaking daycares and schools, the safety, and the access and quality of health care. Moving would be tougher, too. Once the kids were older, we didn't want to uproot them from school if we didn't have to. When they were babies, we just had so much stuff to move. You wouldn't believe how many cribs and how much baby equipment we've donated to church groups when we left a city because it didn't make sense to take things back to Canada and move them again.

I had to consider all of these factors that weren't there before. My life was his life now, too.

* * * * *

Mandy's pregnancy played a big part in my decision to return to Gran Canaria for the 2008–09 season.

I had initially received a strong offer from Barcelona, which would have meant a jump to the EuroLeague with one of the world's best teams and a jump in salary. Gran Canaria was a feeder club at the time. They were usually around the top eight and fighting for a play-off spot, and then their best players would get plucked by the larger-budget teams at the top of the league.

It looked like I was headed to Barcelona, which checked all of our family boxes and even more professional boxes. Instead, Juan Carlos Navarro decided to return from the NBA after his rookie season with Memphis. He'd played for Barcelona before trying the NBA and was coming back, which meant Barcelona didn't feel the need to spend as much money and use an import slot on another guard. It was a surprising move for Navarro and caught me off-guard.

I had other strong offers, but I'd waited on the Barcelona situation to see how it would play out. I was willing to wait on a Barcelona or a Real Madrid, because I didn't know when those situations would open up again and because those teams came with big contracts. There was a risk that other offers would go away, but I had a good backup option. I was coming off a great year in which I was one of the league's top scorers and our team did well, so Gran Canaria wanted to keep me and offered me a raise to stick around.

Mandy was comfortable with the living situation and with the doctors in Las Palmas, so when Barcelona fell through, we decided to stay. I also liked the idea of staying in one place for a while. We'd bounced around so much that stability would be a nice change, and I loved Canaria. I liked the island, I liked the coach, I liked my teammates. It was a good situation all around, with Mandy being due early in the season. It was an exciting time. I was about to have my first child, I was coming off my best season, and now I finally had some familiarity.

We hit the ground running. We lost our opener and then won seven in a row, and I was averaging right around twenty points, near the top of the league again. Right away, I was getting a lot of recognition. It was shaping up as one of the best seasons in years for Gran Canaria.

Coach Salva Maldonado didn't like players averaging twenty points. That may sound strange. His thinking was that a team with eight players who scored ten points was tougher to game-plan for and stop than a team that relied too much on one or two scorers. All I could think was, *What difference does it make? We're winning. Don't mess around with it.* He was worried that if a team stopped me and Joel Freeland, we'd have trouble winning. He wanted to diversify our offence.

I understood the logic, but for me, individually, he was basically telling me my numbers were about to take a big hit. His goal was to win, not to help me get my next contract, and so he took me out of the starting lineup for a little while and cut back my minutes.

I still put up strong numbers for the year. I averaged 15.6 points while playing only twenty-five minutes and shot the ball well. We got to participate in the Copa del Rey, which was an eight-team knockout tournament in February. That was big for the team, because that tournament came with a lot of money and a lot of sponsors. A lot of scouts were there, too, and the fans got really excited for it. Our team cooled off but still ended up finishing sixth in the ACB, which was a good result for Gran Canaria.

We lost in the first round of the ACB playoffs to Unicaja. I'd spent the year almost entirely injury-free and then twisted my ankle pretty badly in the first game of that series and missed the remainder of it.

Even in the playoffs, coaches wouldn't let us play in a game if we hadn't been practising. We had a week in between games, so for a week we did everything we could to get my ankle ready to go. I'd done some ligament damage, which would normally take about four weeks to heal. We were trying to do it in four days. We had great trainers on that team, and I spent the whole week with them. We'd do three hours in the morning, take a break for a few hours, do another three hours in the afternoon, and then do it again at night. We thought if we could get it to where I could put weight on it, I'd be able to tough it out.

These situations could be really tough overseas. I always wanted to play, as a competitor, and teams would often pressure us to play. I took risks and played through things that maybe I wouldn't have if I'd had a guaranteed contract or a long-term deal. Teams looked at us as a piece of meat in some sense, because as import players we were always just rentals. There wasn't a lot of loyalty year to year, so if I pushed an injury and became damaged goods, well, tough luck. There was a lot of money riding on each season, and if I wasn't good to go, they'd find someone who was. It was cutthroat.

I tried everything to play. I wanted to be out there with my team in the playoffs. I carried this tough-guy mentality, told myself, *Don't be a wuss*, and always played through things. It was the same "hockey mentality" I used to bottle up my feelings as a kid. Just put my head down and play. In the long run I did more damage that way, especially with my ankles.

I'd missed one loss already. The series was 1-1, and I felt I would be ready for the third and final game. But if I didn't practise, I couldn't play. That was the way it went there. I wasn't ready in time for our final practice, and I had to sit out the do-or-die game.

We lost, and my season was over. My time in Spain wasn't.

Before I decided that for good, I had to take one more chance at the NBA. The Raptors were calling again.

Carl English dunks the ball during the 3A provincials at Fatima Academy, his last tournament in Newfoundland. The whole community came out to see the game.

A painting of Carl English's old basketball hoop in Patrick's Cove, Newfoundland, which Carl's wife, Mandy, had commissioned as a gift for his birthday.

A dunk contest at University of Hawaii in 1999. Pictured is Carl English jumping over teammate Lance Takaki. Carl won the contest with this dunk.

Carl English at University of Hawaii circa 2000.

In Tulsa, Carl English holds up two awards after winning the Western Athletic Conference (WAC) Championship during his freshman year. One is the championship award, the other the most valuable player (MVP) award. Here his teammates are lifting him up in celebration.

TOP: A montage showing uniforms from all the teams for which Carl English played. This montage was created by Laura González during Carl's time in Gran Canaria, Spain. Laura also created a fan club page for Carl on Facebook @CarlEnglishFansClub.

RIGHT: Carl English playing for Virtus Bologna in First Division against Siena in Italy. Here he is pictured taking a jumpshot.

TOP: Carl English huddles with his AEK Athens teammates.

MIDDLE: Carl English of team Caja Laboral playing against Clay Tucker in the Liga ACB. Carl went on to win the championship with his team.

LEFT: Carl English playing his first year with Virtus Bologna against rival Fortitudo Bologna in Italy.

TOP: Carl English making a move against a defender in Humacao, Puerto Rico.

RIGHT: Carl English of team Caja Laboral playing against Louis Bullock of Real Madrid.

TOP: Carl English after shooting a three-pointer in Tenerife, Spain, during a home game, circa 2015. Carl's opponents were not pleased.

RIGHT: Carl English taking a jumpshot while playing for Alba Berlin in Germany.

LEFT: Carl English playing for Tenerife against Estudiantes. RIGHT: Carl English playing for Gran Canaria during his first year in Spain. Here he is playing in Gran Canaria, Spain, against Mirza Teletović, who later went on to the NBA. Carl and Mirza were teammates two years later.

Carl English of Team Canada opposite Kobe Bryant of the US Dream Team in Las Vegas, 2008.

A big hero for a little school

Everyone at Fatima Academy and along the Cape Shore is 'right out of their minds' over Carl English

BY JOHN BROWNE
The Telegram

Today's "Hawaii Day" at Fatima Academy in honour of the St. Bride's school's favourite son.

Carl English will suit up for the biggest game of his basketball career tonight in Dayton, Ohio and no one is more excited than the people on the Cape Shore.

The 20-year-old from Patrick's Cove, Placentia Bay and his University of Hawaii Rainbow Warriors go up against the Syracuse Orangemen in an NCAA tournament first-rounder. The game will be carried on CTV Sportsnet (Channel 50) approximately 11:30 p.m. and possibly on CBS (Channel 22), which will broadcast either the midwest contest or a south regional game.

The entire student body of 223 at Fatima gathered in the school's gym Thursday just before noon to hear a live national CBC radio interview with English. Every time English mentioned his old school or his hometown a cheer went up.

Carl English

"The people here are right out of their minds over this," said Fatima Academy principal Gordon Pike. "But people here are that way about basketball all the time."

Aloha Fatima!

The students have been encouraged to wear Hawaiian shirts and Warrior colors at school today.

"He's (English) a role model for sure, and you can't forget Jenine (Browne) either," Pike said, referring to the Atlantic universities women's rookie of the year and Fatima graduate who plays for Memorial Sea-Hawks.

"We take great pride in being a very small, out-of-the-way place that can compete with the best of 'em."

Pike, English's high school basketball coach, says he knew his most famous protege would be something special, even if some people had their doubts.

"It's nice to see this happen for him," said Pike, who coached English from Grade 7 to 11.

"He was a good kid. He might have seemed a little cocky on the floor, but he was always very humble. If he's still cocky on the floor it's a matter of survival ... his way of coping with what was going on around him, especially in the American game."

Pike says English remains close to the people of the Cape Shore. He calls often to ask about what's going on or for a little advice.

"He'll never forget his roots," said Pike, who took a phone call from English Thursday afternoon.

"He's working on getting focused for (tonight's game). The team's been looking over tapes of Syracuse, and English has been particularly studying three players he may have to work against."

Pike said the only thing the coaching staff at Fatima can take credit for is introducing English to the game.

"We gave him the opportunity to play but he was a natural ... a special talent. He knew right from the start what he wanted to be and he's very independent," says Pike who believes English has a good chance to play in the NBA one day.

"I've never doubted it. He's got his sights set on where he wants to go and he has lots of confidence now."

English will back up starter Mike McIntyre for the 17-3 Warriors, who are seeded No. 12 in their bracket against the No. 5 seed Orangemen (24-8).

English has had an up and down season. He's gone from seldom-used reserve to Western Athletic Conference (WAC) tournament most valuable player in a span of one month.

> "He (Carl English) was a good kid. He might have seemed a little cocky on the floor, but he was always very humble ... he'll never forget his roots."
>
> *Gordon Pike,
> principal and basketball coach,
> Fatima Academy*

His basket with 1.8 seconds left in regulation that sent last Saturday's WAC final against Tulsa Golden Hurricanes into overtime is being called one of the biggest shots in UH history. The Warriors eventually won the game 78-72 with English scoring 25 points off the bench, including seven in overtime.

The six-foot-four redshirt freshman guard has been in the media spotlight since then.

"I'm not going to let it get to my head," English told the Honolulu Advertiser earlier this week.

"I think that could have been anybody on this team. That's what's good about us. Any one of us can step in and do the job, and we all have confidence in each other.

"It feels good, and I think we deserve it. But we gotta keep going, put everything together and get a couple wins out of this. We can't just accept being here, we gotta do something with it."

Wanted man

English's road roommate, Phil Martin, a native of Hamilton, Ont., said the phone in their room has been ringing a lot in the past few days, but hardly ever for him.

"Yeah, they always ask for Carl," he said. "But that's cool. He got his chance to shine, and now everybody wants to talk to him about it."

The Warriors are loaded with experience at shooting guard and small forward, so English (4.7 ppg, 1.6 apg and 2.9 rpg.) will have to wait his turn, despite his obvious talent and desire.

"I think he's going to be a great player for us," assistant coach Bob Nash told the Star-Bulletin.

"He's just got to get under control. He's excitable and has a lot of energy," head coach Riley Wallace added.

"He makes things happen, which is good."

Peter English, Carl's oldest brother, now a construction worker in Orangeville, Ont., is making the trip to Dayton in a minivan with relatives.

What Carl doesn't know, according to Pike, is that his girlfriend Mandy will be a passenger in that van.

"We're hoping that won't throw him off," Pike said with a laugh.

Back in October, six-foot-four Patrick's Cove native Carl English (23) flew over five-foot-four Lance Takaki on his way winning the University of Hawaii's slam-dunk contest. These days, English (who no longer keeps his head shaved) is still soaring as a member of the underdog Rainbow Warriors, who take on Syracuse University today in the opening round of the NCAA basketball tournament.

DENNIS ODA/ THE HONOLULU STAR-BULLETIN

Hero in Hawaii

Europe may be English's best route to NBA

Island HOPPER

Carl English, with girlfriend Mandy Dohey, can hardly stand to watch as the NBA draft unfolded last night.

have to seize it."

English had another year of eligibility at the University of Hawaii — despite the fact that he's already graduated with a liberal arts degree — and could have worked on his game, in the sun, for another season with the Rainbow Warriors.

NBA draft veteran Jamaal Magloire stopped by, waded into crowd around English, and offered a few words of encouragement.

"I've watched this kid on TV and there's no doubt he can play at the next level," Magloire offered last night. "I know he wanted to get drafted tonight, but the bottom line is being with a team in October.

"All it takes is one team to invite you to camp."

English was surrounded by his family and friends — his Aunt Betty was there from Newfoundland, as was his girlfriend, Mandy Dohey, and a boisterous bunch of his brothers and cousins — but the night was almost as much about who wasn't there as who was.

Uncle Junior McGrath, who raised English as his own, is now deceased. And Kevin and Lavinia English, Carl's mom and dad, had long ago passed away.

"It's always something that you think about, but this is a joy-

house fire on Good Friday in 1986. Junior McGrath and his wife, Betty, took him into their home and raised him. Then, two summers ago, McGrath died, while English was home for the summer and just after they'd finished a day on the water, fishing for cod and crab.

"People, especially from home, say Junior would have loved to be here," Dohey said, looking around the club. "We were all just talking about that. It's obviously in his head. Junior was one of his biggest fans. I'm sure he'd have loved to be here. And obviously we'd love for him to be

It was Junior McGrath who helped English nail a backboard and rim to a post on Route 100, a busy highway outside their home. And it was on the blacktop where English honed the skills that led him to the University of Hawaii and, last night, to the dream of a career in the NBA.

Scouts describe English as fearless. That's a quality you learn when the basketball court you practised on as a kid was known locally as Route 100, and which ran right through Patrick's Cove.

TOP LEFT: Carl English clapping to the fans after a win for Gran Canaria. This was just after Carl's son, Ryder, was born, and the crowd gave him a standing ovation.

TOP RIGHT: Carl English playing for DKV Joventut in Badalona, Spain, 2011.

BOTTOM RIGHT: Carl English of team Caja Laboral in Vitoria, Spain, poses for a pre-season photo shoot.

TOP: Carl English's Team Canada jersey and silver medal from the 2015 Pan Am Games.

RIGHT: Carl English of Team Canada guarding against Kobe Bryant of the US Dream Team in 2009.

RIGHT: Carl English takes a jumpshot over his opponent while playing for Estudiantes Madrid, circa 2012.

BOTTOM: A headshot of Carl English that was taken while he was playing for Spanish team DKV Joventut.

TOP: Carl English takes a jumpshot against Windsor while playing for the St. John's Edge upon his first year returning home.

RIGHT: Carl English gives back to the community by reviving the basketball courts at St. John Bosco. Pictured is Carl playing one-on-one with a student from the school.

Carl English instructing students on how to stretch
at his kids' camp, CE23 Basketball School.

For community outreach and to gain a better understanding of young people with challenges of all kinds, Carl English plays a scrimmage with other athletes during the Special Olympics and Paralympics. Pictured here with Carl is Alex Wells.

Shoes worn by Carl English that were designed by kids at the Janeway Children's Hospital. After Carl played while wearing the shoes, they were auctioned off and sold to a fan for several thousand dollars, which was donated back to the Janeway.

Family photo. Carl and Mandy English in their backyard with their three children, (L-R) Ryder, Kirsten, and Kylie.

LEFT: Carl English of the St. John's Edge proudly displaying the New-foundland flag on his uniform.

BOTTOM: Carl English of the St. John's Edge takes a shot from the free-throw line, 2018. The shot went in. Photo by Jeff Parsons.

13

ALWAYS ALMOST. OVERSEAS III.

THE RAPTORS ALWAYS MADE THE most sense if I was going to make it to the NBA.

The story writes itself. By the summer of 2009, I had established myself overseas and things were finally lining up for me. The team had moved on from Sam Mitchell and made Jay Triano the head coach, and we had a great relationship from the national program. Between Coach Triano and Maurizio Gherardini, I had two big supporters in important positions.

I agreed to go to Summer League with the Raptors with the belief that a strong showing would land me a contract.

Summer League was early enough in the off-season that there wasn't quite as much risk of missing out on overseas offers, and I had some leverage coming off a few strong seasons. In Europe, I was the guy teams were chasing to sign in June. Those deals weren't there in October. I'd made it clear to teams that I wouldn't go to an NBA training camp without a guarantee, so overseas teams knew my decision wouldn't drag on too long.

I thought my time trying to make the NBA was behind me entirely. I'd started enjoying Europe and making good money, and I was still frustrated with how my earlier close calls with the NBA had played out. I'd always had it in the back of my mind that I hadn't gotten a full shot. I was always torn in that way, because I didn't want to give up on the NBA dream, but I also felt I shouldn't have to try out. Coach Triano and the Raptors made too much sense not to try one more time.

The Raptors had drafted DeMar DeRozan that summer, and he was set to make his debut in Summer League. Their roster for Las Vegas also had Roko Ukić, a young guard they'd brought over the year before, a couple of other players with a legitimate chance to crack the roster, and a handful of journeymen. I was playing well in our camp leading up to Summer League and thought I had made a strong impression.

Baskonia (or TAU Ceramica, as they were also known) called and came after me hard while I was with the Raptors. They were a EuroLeague team and consistently one of the best teams in Spain. In the Spanish ACB league, teams like Barcelona and Real Madrid were at the top of the pyramid for prestige and money, and Baskonia came right after.

I had a large contract offer that my agents were pressuring me to sign. I kept trying to hold them off a little longer. Justin thought I was crazy. I told him, "Man, I'm here in Las Vegas now. I want to do this. I'm not going to sign until I figure out the Raptors stuff. I feel like I can do this."

Summer League was set to start on July 10. On July 9, the Raptors shook up their roster with a massive trade. They were initially going to sign Hedo Türkoğlu as a free agent, which wouldn't have had much of an impact on me since we didn't play the same position. The deal got bigger and bigger, though, and it ended up as this big four-team, double sign-and-trade that involved eight players, picks, and a bunch of cash flying around. Because of the way the deal was structured, the Raptors also took on Devean George and Antoine Wright.

It was a huge deal for the Raptors. Türkoğlu was the biggest free agent signing they'd made. It ended up being a really bad fit, and they traded him the next year, but at the time they'd thought it was a game changer.

It threw everything into confusion for me. The Raptors now had more players and less financial flexibility, and they were going to have to make some other moves to balance out the roster. The spot that I was initially going to be competing for against Quincy Douby might not have existed any longer, and they couldn't guarantee me anything until they figured out the rest of their moves.

Coach Triano was honest with me about it. I'd kept him in the loop on my talks with Baskonia, and he didn't want me to miss an opportunity because I was in the dark about their plans. He said, "Carl, I know you, I know what you've got on the table. We have to trim our team now. My advice is to take the job in Vitoria."

The NBA had always been in my head, but over time I'd been able to shift my focus to the international game and make the most of those chances. I felt that the more I let the NBA go, the more success I had overseas. It still weighed on me at times, especially during that first year in Italy. It got easier by the year. I was a rock star as a top player in Spain, the money's better, and my family was with me. I came to accept it, but I couldn't make peace with it.

Chasing the NBA dream for so long was draining. It was completely exhausting. I'm a person who keeps things inside and puts my head down and works, so my approach was always to figure out the next step and work hard to get there. Those failures motivated me. I always looked in the mirror to see what I could do differently.

I also never took a proper off-season to work on my game. It was always camps and Summer League and the national team. After a while, all of the missed chances and close calls add up.

I was twenty-eight years old and on my seventh summer of trying to make the NBA. I wasn't putting myself through that anymore. I took Coach Triano's advice and the advice of my agent, signed the deal with Baskonia, and left Vegas the day that Summer League began.

* * * * *

That off-season was a whirlwind between Toronto, Baskonia, the 2009 FIBA Americas Championship in Puerto Rico, and Mandy's second pregnancy.

Ryder had been born in November, and Mandy was due again in the winter. We hadn't wasted any time. We always joked about how quickly it happened again.

Signing with Baskonia was as much of a family decision as it was a financial and basketball decision. The guaranteed money came into my thinking, of course. It was a safety net for me and my family and with what we were building our lives. There was more to it than that. Because Mandy was pregnant and we had the baby, we had to make sure wherever we ended up was as good a situation as with Gran Canaria in terms of doctors and support. Looking ahead, we wanted to be in a nice city with good schools.

Vitoria-Gasteiz fit all of the criteria. It's a beautiful city. They put us up in an amazing house. Baskonia was a terrific basketball fit, too.

I'd almost signed with Baskonia the season before. In February, we'd agreed to a deal that would have paid me the most I'd ever made in my career. The hook was that it was based on my being able to get a passport for a European or a Cotonou country (mostly former colonies of European countries whose passports didn't count as imports). If I could get one of those passports by helping build up one of the local basketball federations, I wouldn't count as an import player and would make more money.

That deal didn't get signed because they couldn't get me a passport. We stayed in contact, and they still offered more than a lot of other teams. They were a EuroLeague team trying to build a powerhouse. We agreed on a one-and-one deal, which was a contract for one year with a mutual option for a second year.

I was already in great shape from gearing up for the Raptors and playing with the national team. I had a good camp and was comfortable right away. I was familiar with Spain, and Spanish fans were familiar with me. Vitoria-Gasteiz didn't have as strong a soccer culture as other Spanish cities, so basketball was huge there. I did a few endorsements. Stardom in a city like that was a lot of fun.

The coach, Duško Ivanović, had a reputation for being tough and strict, but I found him to be fair. He didn't have any favourites, so I was treated the same as Tiago Splitter and Mirza Teletović, who were treated the same as the guys further down the depth chart. Our roster was loaded, which helped. Everyone understood that we were strong and deep, which meant sacrificing minutes and touches. Our second team was as good as our first.

That hurt my numbers, but it didn't bother me as much as it had earlier in my career. I was established now, and teams would know my minutes and scoring numbers were down because of the good quality of our team. I shot the ball well, too, so even though I averaged nine points, I was doing it in only twenty minutes, and doing it efficiently.

I was broken down by the end of the year. My ankle had been acting up again most of the season, and I was playing at less than a hundred per cent. That was manageable. What happened in the play-offs wasn't.

I was taking a shot in our final game of the ACB regular season, and a defender closed out on me. Going up for a shot leaves your midsection wide open and unprotected. The defender closed out hard and pierced my rib cage. I cracked two ribs.

I sat out the first round, which we swept, 2-0, as well as the first game of the second round. I came back for game two of that second-round series against Madrid and played every game the rest of the way. My role was a lot smaller once I was back. The team had won three straight playoff games without me and I wasn't a hundred per cent, so I'd mostly come in to shoot off the bench, bang a couple of threes, and go sit down. My numbers went down, but we were winning.

Our depth ended up saving us all year. We were hit hard by injuries. At one point we had six players out at once. It was tough to stay competitive in a league as good as Spain's with that many injuries. All of our injured players returned late in the year, which gave us a boost for the stretch run. We'd finished second in the ACB standings thanks to a late push and were able to cope with my injury, and we beat Madrid once I was back.

Then we swept Barcelona to win the ACB championship.

* * * * *

That year was incredible, both on and off the court. On December 3, Mandy gave birth to our first daughter, Kirsten.

Being able to spend that season with my wife and two children was something for which I was very grateful. I didn't know what to expect with fatherhood until I had my kids. I would look at them, each one, and think, *This little person is fifty per cent made up of me*, and I could see myself in them. It's an amazing feeling to come home to that.

Mandy carried a heavy burden that year with a toddler and a newborn. My season was hectic and exhausting from the amount of practice at that high a level, and Mandy was terrific with the kids. It made for a funny living situation with my hours around games and the hours that babies sleep.

We had a master bedroom in this beautiful house, and we put all the beds together in there. We had a king, two queens, and a twin all pushed together from wall to wall so that our bedroom was just one giant bed. We'd start off the night with the kids in bed with us, and I'd just roll over to the other side of this enormous bed when I needed to sleep. The night before a game, I'd go to a different bedroom because I'd get home late and need a proper sleep.

Having a girl was much different than having a boy. That's something that comes up once they get a little older, but I could sense it even when I was holding them as babies. With Ryder, I'm rough and tumble. With Kirsten, and later when we had Kylie, I'm more dainty, singing and dancing with them and letting them do makeup on me. I grew up with four brothers and then joined a house with three male cousins and only one girl. Having little girls around was a big adjustment.

We spent most of that summer home in Newfoundland so everyone could see the kids. Mandy took them back a little earlier while I was still in the playoffs, and then I met up with them after we won the championship. It was my first real off-season, because I wasn't doing Summer League or mini-camps and I had to miss the World Championships for Team Canada to heal my ribs. I was disappointed to miss that tournament, but it was a great opportunity to recharge and spend time with my family.

When Ryder was born, that shifted my priorities when deciding on future contracts. With two kids at such a young age, I started thinking about stability and consistency. I knew growing up bouncing around would have some challenges, so I did my best to make sure I put them first as much as I could. Health care and education wherever we went were important, and because both of them had been born in Spain and were Spanish, I had a preference to stay there.

Later in my career, I tried other countries and loved them. After the season in Baskonia, where my numbers were down and I'd finished the year banged up, I still had offers outside of Spain. My best move might have been to go to a EuroLeague team in Greece, where I'd always received a lot of interest. Olympiacos and Panathinaikos had reached out, and knowing what I know now, they would have been good places to land. CSKA Moscow in Russia was another. The most aggressive team was Galatasaray, a Turkish team that was trying to load up to try to move from second to first division, but I didn't think moving to a second-division team, even for first-division money, was the right move.

I probably should have taken the jump and left Spain for bigger offers with bigger teams. But we were so comfortable with Spain as far as health care and the language and culture that I opted to stay there for the foreseeable future.

* * * * *

I ended up signing with Joventut, who had produced players like Ricky Rubio and Rudy Fernández, for the 2010–11 season.

They'd had a rough season the year before in the ACB and fell out of EuroCup, so it was a step back in terms of team quality but a good opportunity to have another season where my role was bigger and my numbers were strong.

Their coach, Pepu Hernández, was also a big draw for me. He'd won a World Championship as Spain's head coach in 2006 and had a reputation as someone who put players and their families first. It was rare in Europe for a coach to ask about my apartment, my kids, and my home life before talking basketball. Other coaches wanted players to leave all of that at home. Coach Hernández was a great coach and an even better person.

Joventut is based in Badalona, which is just outside of Barcelona, and they had a fun rivalry with Barcelona. Barcelona was the big-budget, big-city team, and Joventut was the underdog. Their games were referred to as the Catalan basketball derby, and fans kept track of which side was winning the all-time head-to-head. The Spanish fans all knew the other teams well, and that added a fun element to games on the road.

The province of Catalonia is a beautiful place to live. My family was comfortable and happy. I was so used to Spain by then that there was no adjustment to a new city. Other than some bankruptcy issues the team was going through, everything about the transition away from the court was smooth.

It took me a little while to adjust to my role under Coach Hernández. Due to passport loopholes, we had a lot of Americans on our team, and the start of the year was challenging for everyone trying to figure out the pecking order. I took a step back initially to let that work itself out and find my place. A few weeks in, we were struggling, and so I started to push a little bit more as a leader on and off the court.

We got hot and climbed as high as fifth place. We looked like we might make the playoffs. We'd qualified for the Copa del Rey, and the whole city was getting behind us. I was putting up some big numbers again, too. I had a pair of thirty-point games and won a Player of the Week and then Player of the Month for January. I was getting noticed once again, and offers were coming in for next year already. It felt like I was back where I needed to be.

All of that momentum stopped in late January.

A few weeks before, I had fallen and hurt my right wrist in practice. My legs were taken out, and I caught myself awkwardly when landing. An MRI didn't show anything, so I taped it up and only did cardio each week to try to get ready for the next game. I thought I was dealing with a minor injury, so I just loaded up on ibuprofen and taped myself up on game day. I was putting up twenty-five- and thirty-point nights with my wrist banged up and thought it was nothing.

I fell again in a game and knew something more serious was going on. I stopped taking ibuprofen because I thought it might be masking something. They sent me for a second MRI, this time a contrast MRI so they could see each individual ligament and tendon. That was on a

Friday, and the hope was that I'd be cleared for Sunday's game. On Saturday, the doctors called and told me that I needed emergency surgery to save a ligament in my wrist.

My season was over, and so was Joventut's. We fell out of the playoff race and finished thirteenth in the league. My bounce-back season was cut off after seventeen games during one of the hottest streaks of my career.

* * * * *

The one bright side of the injury was that it forced me to take time to heal and recover.

I hadn't had surgery since my redshirt year of college and had always played through smaller injuries, especially with my ankles. When I first went to Joventut, I failed the medical because of the condition of my ankles. I practised for Coach Hernández, and he said, "This guy is what we need. We'll look past it." My body had adjusted to years of ankle damage, and I was still fast and athletic, doing 360 dunks or windmills, whatever I wanted. They ignored the medical, even though the MRI of my ankles looked terrible, because I looked good on the court.

When I went in for wrist surgery, I stayed in the hospital to have surgery on my ankle, too. I paid 8,000 euros out of my own pocket to get that done because it was a pre-existing injury. Joventut was dealing with some bankruptcy issues, and once I was hurt, I became a lower priority to get paid. It took me nearly two years to get the rest of the guaranteed money on my contract. It added additional stress to the regular stress of an injury.

And now my outlook for 2011 was unclear because I'd be coming off of two surgeries.

Getting one surgery right after the other probably wasn't the smartest thing. I was thinking in terms of rehab timelines. If I did them both at once, I could be back sooner than if I'd had one surgery, rehabbed, and then had the other.

Going through one surgery, let alone two, is a grind, psychologically. Once you're done with a team, you're done. You're just a player to them. There was a great deal of uncertainty that weighed on me going through the surgeries alone, without a team behind me. I didn't know if I was going to get back to where I was as a player. I didn't know if ligament damage in my shooting wrist would affect my shot or if another surgery on my ankle would limit my athleticism. I didn't know if I'd be able to move, cut, jump, shoot.

I didn't know where my next contract was going to come from or if teams would see me as damaged goods. It was sad. I had my family at home, but I was all alone in my mind.

The rehab process after those two surgeries was long. I had to adjust my shooting form because of my wrist. It didn't go back the same way that it used to, and I couldn't get that same snap with it, so I had to change how I got my shot off. That takes a lot of time to rebuild. Any shooter will tell you that mechanics are part of it but the mental side is just as big. Not only did I have to get my shot back, I had to get my confidence back and regain my ability to get to my spots.

That depended on my ankle. I could move well enough after the surgery, but I didn't get the same jump back. After my ankle surgery in college, I was dunking right away. After this one, I didn't jump the same again. I had to change and adjust my game, all while I was trying to get healthy.

I'd been in the prime of my career in Europe, and now I was starting all over again. Everything overseas operated on what a player could do for a team *right now*. I was only as good as what I could offer for one year. I was coming off two surgeries, and nobody had seen me play since, so it didn't matter that I'd been putting up Player of the Month performances and shooting well the last time I played. The offers I had were less than they would have been otherwise, because I was a shooting specialist and teams didn't know if I could shoot anymore.

I was healthy enough by the end of August to go with Team Canada to the 2011 Tuto Marchand Cup in Brazil and the Americas Championship in Argentina. That was a great opportunity to shake off the rust and get my confidence back after not playing for over seven months.

I also got to show teams I could still shoot. I led our team in scoring and hit forty-five per cent of my threes. We finished sixth, which wasn't a bad finish, considering how young we were with guys like Cory Joseph and Kelly Olynyk playing as twenty-year-olds.

From there I went to Seville. They were coming off of a losing season and were willing to take a chance on me with some assurances. My contract had a clause that said if my left ankle or right wrist were reinjured and I missed a certain amount of time, my deal would be voided. I was comfortable with it because I felt good by then.

Seville was another great Spanish city to live in. It's in the south, so the weather was beautiful, and the city is full of historic architecture and culture.

It wasn't a great basketball situation. The coach, Joan Plaza, had recruited me hard and told me everything I wanted to hear. When I got there, I was battling for playing time the whole season. It was like being back in Virtus, where my minutes would jump around game to game, and he wasn't sure how he wanted to use me. I hit over forty per cent of my threes for the year, but my numbers looked unimpressive because I only averaged sixteen minutes and I wasn't attacking the rim as well as I had before the surgery.

The team was happy with how things had gone. I had a crucial role on the team, and we got back to the playoffs, and I'd helped mentor a couple of the team's young players, like Tomáš Satoranský and Kristaps Porziņģis.

I wasn't as happy. My production was down, and coming off of the surgeries, I didn't know where I would go next. When I left, I told the coach, "I did everything you asked me to do. You told me what I wanted to hear, and it never translated to the court." I told him I felt we could have made a deeper playoff run if he had used me more. He apologized, but in his eyes the season had been a success.

It had. I just felt like I was right back where I was the summer before.

* * * * *

Estudiantes was in as tough a spot as me.

They were supposed to have fallen out of the first division that summer, but Tenerife, who were going to come up to replace them, didn't have enough money. Estudiantes avoided relegation because of finances. That was crucial. Some of the lower-end teams would celebrate avoiding relegation at the end of the season or sign a player late in the year to move up a spot or two in the standings and save their season. Estudiantes hung on because Tenerife didn't have the money. They got lucky and wanted to bounce back.

Txus Vidorreta was their coach, and he recruited me. He had a similar style and reputation to Coach Hernández as a great player's coach. Madrid, where Estudiantes was based, was an attractive option for my family, with good English schools and plenty for the kids to do. It checked all of our boxes and would be an opportunity for me to play big minutes and re-establish my value, so that's where I signed.

I tore it up. In the middle of the season, I was leading the ACB league in scoring and had won four Player of the Week awards and a Player of the Month.

I received offers to leave Estudiantes to join a bigger club. Barcelona had made a serious offer to come buy me out of my deal with Estudiantes and relocate there. That happened sometimes. There were no trades in those leagues, so a richer team or a winning team would try to buy a player out from a lower-budget team or a losing team.

I was technically free to go because Estudiantes was behind on paying me. If a team was late on payment for a month, a player could leave. They had run into money trouble, and sometimes the gym would have no heat or they'd miss payments to players. But I still didn't want to leave that situation. I was playing so well, I loved Coach Vidorreta, and we had a great group of guys like Lucas Nogueira and Germán Gabriel and Kyle Kuric. The move from Madrid to Barcelona wouldn't have been too bad, but my wife and kids were happy where we were.

If Barcelona had given me a second year on a contract, I would have gone, because then I'd have known I wouldn't have to move my family again. I had my agent tell them I'd take a little less in the second year to get that security. They were in a situation where a lot of changes were going to be made that summer, so they couldn't commit.

I decided to stay where I was. I looked at it this way: *I'm going to put my head down and I'm going to dominate, and then in the summer I'll sign that mega-contract.* That's how I thought it would play out. I went back to playing, and my agent started working on deals for the following season, which were already starting to pick up.

I should have left. It was a good team and a jump back to Euro-League, and my career was about to shift.

* * * * *

With about six weeks left in the year, I had to go into the hospital for a couple of days. I'd gotten rundown and was feeling drained, so the team made me check in to recover. I've always had what's called a tachycardia arrhythmia, and the worry was that it might have something to do with that.

With tachycardia arrhythmia, my heart rate hits 220–230 at odd times. Before I signed with Estudiantes, I'd passed their physical, but the Olympics committee that ran other tests wouldn't sign off on me. The club was pushing for the doctors to clear me, because none of the tests showed anything wrong. With that particular condition, it wasn't about my response when exercising; my heart rate can just jump for no reason. They ended up putting me on a baby-dose of a beta blocker to control the arrhythmia.

When they discovered the arrhythmia, they made me get checked out in more detail. There was a specialist based in Newfoundland, Dr. Connors, who called me.

"There's this type of special arrhythmia," he said. "There's a place, I'm not sure if you know about it, called Patrick's Cove."

"Yeah, I'm from there," I said.

"Well, there's this man that's the leading candidate for all my research. His name is Junior McGrath."

"He's my uncle."

"You have to come see me right away."

He thought Uncle Junior was my uncle through blood, and maybe we had the same condition. Uncle Junior's condition was rare, so if I had it, too, I'd be a candidate for Dr. Connors's research and might be at higher risk.

I explained that he wasn't my blood relative. He said, "He was really proud of you. As soon as he woke up from surgery, he asked about you. He kept your picture at the bottom of the bed." That was touching to hear. I'd had a scare with my arrhythmia, not knowing how it might affect everything else, and I felt in that moment like Uncle Junior and I were still connected.

Luckily, it turned out the reason I was in the hospital had nothing to do with my arrhythmia. They said my white blood cells were a little low and I had been trying to play through the flu. It was nothing major.

I was coming back from this bad case of the flu, and we were playing against Manresa. Troy DeVries, their top scorer, was chasing me for the ACB scoring title, so I was trying to lock him up defensively. I followed him toward a screen, and when I tried to fight around it, his big man, a six-foot-eleven American named Josh Asselin, stepped in with his hip.

I hit my shoulder on his hip and knew right away it was bad.

The shoulder popped out. I was lying on the floor telling the trainers to pop it back in, but they couldn't. I had torn my entire shoulder. I dislocated my AC joint and tore ligaments all through the shoulder.

They took me off the court and to the locker room, and I broke down in the shower. I was crying and didn't care if anyone saw. I wasn't in physical pain; I couldn't even feel anything, really. But I knew how bad it was and that everything I'd worked for was down the drain, all because I'd gotten caught on a screen the wrong way.

The whole premise of the season was to stick with the plan, dominate with Estudiantes, and get to the end of the year without any injuries. I was leading the best league outside of the NBA in scoring, I was getting offers from Turkey and Barcelona, and there was NBA interest again. Whatever happened, I was in for a big summer and a big raise. Now I was hurt again off of another freak injury, just like with the wrist. All of that crashed down on me in the moment. I was a wreck.

I called Mandy, screeching. She was watching the game at home that day because one of the kids was sick, and we both just started crying on the phone.

Mandy has always played such an instrumental role in moments like these. An injury is the hardest thing to go through as an athlete. I had support from doctors and from fans, but mostly I was alone. Mandy was always my rock through those situations. To have her to confide in when things were bad was so important, because I would never show frustration or pain or sadness with anyone else. A lot of stress comes from that, and she always kept me grounded. She always understood. She knew when I needed to let it out and scream or cry.

And man, I was crying.

Coach Vidorreta came in upset, and he knew how upset I was. He picked me up and said he'd do whatever he could to help me get healthy. He knew what this injury meant. Everyone knew how much this season meant at this stage in my career.

It was likely that my best season was over.

* * * * *

It was a grade three AC joint injury, which is a complete separation of the joint that can sometimes require surgery. To avoid another surgery, I opted to let it heal and strengthen all the ligaments with rehab.

I went home and cleared my head, then came back to train. My goal was to make it back and finish the season, even if it was just for the last two games. I wanted to show teams I was healthy. I nearly made it back for our second-to-last game. I pushed myself extremely hard, trying to make it back for that last game.

I had to play, and play well. I wanted to go into the off-season with everyone knowing I was healthy. If a player led the ACB in scoring, usually that meant an NBA deal or a million-dollar contract in Europe. I wanted to make sure my stock was where it should be and there were no injury concerns. I had only one more game to show that.

My conditioning was already back in decent shape, but I had to show in practice that I was game ready. We had a practice the night before our final game, and I pushed hard to make sure my cardio would be where it needed to be the next day.

I went up for a dunk, and when I landed, I felt something in my back. My back locked up, and I couldn't straighten up. I could touch my toes, but I couldn't stand up straight. They had to give me an epidural just to straighten out. I went to the game the next day and could barely move.

I was still pushing to play, not knowing how serious it was. The pain in my back slowly went away, and then my leg started shutting down. My quad was seizing up. I tried doing a leg press and couldn't even do five pounds. I was struggling to walk.

I'd herniated two discs in my back.

14

CANADIAN PRIDE. NATIONAL TEAM.

THROUGH ALL OF THE UPS AND DOWNS with the NBA and the moves around Europe, the one constant in my professional career was the Canadian national team. I would head home to New-foundland briefly after the season, do whatever tryouts or camps I had that summer, then join Team Canada for whatever was on the sched-ule for that summer.

That was no different now that I was hurt. After I herniated the two discs in my back and started having trouble with my legs, I went to see Alex McKechnie. Alex was one of the biggest and best names in sports science and was involved with the Canada pro-gram, so I had the luxury of going to him for rehab. When I saw him, he told me I was six to eight months away from being able to play, if I was lucky.

I said, "I can't be. I'll be fine. You can't be telling me this right now." There was a lot going through my head in that moment. I was heading into the biggest off-season of my career, coming off a season as Spain's leading scorer, with dozens of offers, and now another injury nobody knew about.

I also wanted to play for Canada that summer, because the 2013

FIBA Americas Championship was a qualifying tournament for the 2014 World Cup.

Since joining the Canadian program in 2000, our goal was to build to get back to the Olympics. They'd gone in 2000 with Steve Nash, and we'd failed to qualify since. Those of us who went through those lean years together kept the focus on getting back there, and as the younger wave of Canadian NBA talent came up, we thought we were getting close. The Olympics was one of my career goals, and a World Cup berth would help us get there. After over a decade in the program, I didn't want to miss that window.

Alex told me I needed six to eight months, but I was going to be ready for Canada camp in four or five. Playing for Canada meant that much to me.

* * * * *

When I first suited up for Canada at the under-twenty-one games in 2000, I didn't have that sense of pride playing for the national team yet. I did it that summer because I needed an outlet after Uncle Junior's death, and I thought he would have wanted me to play. It was a way to get on the court and escape.

In my college years, I missed out on the chance to play with Steve to help at home with the catch in the summer of 2002. My family had to come first, even though that would have been a tremendous experience, to play with Steve and under Jay Triano. The summer of 2003 was Steve's last time playing for the national program, and I regretted not playing that year.

I just did what the team and the people around me suggested. I was an undrafted rookie trying to make the Pacers, and that's where I focused. It was still hard to get rookies and young players into the senior program because of team and agent influence.

Those were two missed opportunities to play with Steve and possibly qualify for the Olympics, and it took us a long time to get back to that point. With the type of person and player Steve was, and how willing a teacher and leader he was, those summers would have helped me a lot early in my career. Knowing what I know now, I would have played without question. But the way it played out, I didn't suit up until Steve had retired from the national team.

I was always a very proud Newfoundlander and a proud Canadian, but until I represented my country, I don't think I truly knew how special that experience was. Once I got a taste of playing for my country, it became one of the most important things in my career.

The chance to wear a Canada jersey was a tremendous honour. I took a lot of pride in being one of the best players from my country and being one of the only people to represent the Atlantic provinces on the international basketball level. I felt I had the province, and that entire part of Canada, on my back.

I'd go to international events and see the sacrifices other players made for their countries, too, and that inspired me more. I remember watching Jorge Garbajosa wear a sneaker one size up right after he'd had surgery, because he'd swell up so much and refused to sit out. There's a passion to the international game that was contagious. Once I experienced those tournaments and those moments and what it was like to fight as a team for my country, I wanted to do it every chance I got.

I always played such a large role with Canada that it helped my game, too. It meant a camp and a tournament playing with and against the best players in the world. I was the captain of the team for seven years, so it helped me grow as a teammate and as a leader as well.

The best part about playing for Canada was the camaraderie. I forged relationships that lasted my whole career, spending my summers travelling around the world with teammates who became close friends. Jesse Young and I would play pranks on other guys or we'd get into food fights on the road. A couple of times we pushed the envelope, especially once I was one of the veterans and would get the young guys going.

I had so many good teammates on those Canada teams. Jesse, Brady Heslip, the Doornekamps, Kyle Wiltjer, Melvin Ejim, Kelly Olynyk, Cory Joseph, Rans Brempong, Levon Kendall, Shep, and Jermaine Anderson were all guys with whom I built life-long bonds. The camaraderie of being on the road in another country with guys you've played with every summer for years is unmatched.

It wasn't just my own teammates, either. I crossed paths with a lot of guys during the season whom I would then go up against in the off-season. We competed against those other countries, but I also developed relationships from seeing guys so often.

The Brazilian national team took a few of us out one time in Brazil. Those guys partied like rock stars when they were at home. It was Jesse, Marcelinho Huertas, Tiago Splitter, and I and a few others, maybe Nenê or Anderson Varejão or Lucas Nogueira. Someone with big hair. We were all in a cab, and two of them hung out the windows, banging on the doors and chanting. We all had to give the cab driver whatever money we had at the end of the ride because they destroyed his car. The Brazilian guys almost got in a fight at a Burger King after that. All I could think was, *Where the hell am I going? Where am I?*

I have so many memories of these fun, bizarre moments that I

A jubilant Carl English and Jesse Young in the Dominican Republic after qualifying for the World Championships. Andy Rautins and Aaron Doornekamp in background.

would never have experienced without playing every summer, and so many friends with whom I would never have gotten as close. Even something like my friendship with Mark Bayne, who started as our Nike rep for Team Canada and became my permanent connection at Nike and a great friend, developed from there. Matt York and Paul Elliott were trainers I built relationships with through Team Canada. Those experiences touched everything. It was a huge part of my career and a huge part of my life.

It was a big commitment, but I don't know many guys who didn't come out of the national team better off for it and having loved the experience.

Eventually, there was no guessing whether I would play if I was healthy. I'd get advice some summers that I should focus on training camps or work on my own game, or that I should rest up. A lot of European teams wanted me to come over early, too, and usually the late-summer tournaments overlapped with European training camps. It didn't matter. If I could play, I was playing.

* * * * *

My first summer with the senior men's team was in 2005. Leo Rautins had just been named the new head coach, and we headed to the Dominican Republic for the FIBA Americas Championship.

Canada Basketball has come a long way since that time. Our camp that summer was at Humber College. We slept in the dorm rooms and didn't have per diem money. To look at the program now, where they fly players first class, put them up in five-star hotels with full buffets, and have much better trainers and training facilities, it shows how much basketball has grown in Canada. I was there through that growth and saw the conditions and the funding and the organization get better every summer.

Back in 2005, the program was rebuilding. Steve Nash had moved on, and our roster wasn't very strong. I was only twenty-four, and there were still seven guys younger than me on the team. Coach Triano had been let go because his vision for what came next didn't fit the program's, although it should have. He wanted to focus on development and building from the youth level up and get the national team out to Summer League to play, things that were ahead of their time for Canada. Instead, it was Coach Rautins's first summer coaching the team.

We went 1-3, which was disappointing, but I led the team in scoring and enjoyed the experience.

Because we finished ninth in that tournament, we failed to qualify for the 2006 World Championship. That summer we played in a handful of exhibition series against teams that were getting ready for the World Championship. We played against Dirk Nowitzki and Germany twice, which was a good experience. I had my best game for Canada up to that point, scoring thirty-four points against Serbia and Montenegro. We tried to use those games against bigger teams as a way to start building.

I always found a lot of value in playing against better countries, even in exhibitions. Every chance to work on my game was valuable. Whether it was a tournament or a tune-up, it was usually late in summer, which helped me get ready for the upcoming season. I knew there were a lot of factors that led to guys not playing for their national teams, but I always used it as part of my off-season plan to build up for the coming year.

The summer of 2007 was a lot of fun. I played well in the Tuto Marchand Cup in Puerto Rico as a tune-up for the Americas Championship. Coach Rautins was one of the best motivators in settings like that. He was good about letting his staff handle the tactics, and he focused on getting us riled up. He'd make these pre-game speeches like he was ready to go out there and fight with us, and he had a lot of good stories from his time playing. He was always inspiring.

We played against Argentina in Puerto Rico, and the benches cleared at one point. I had thirty points in a win, and things got really chippy. International basketball was always a little dirtier. Argentina took some liberties with us, I think because we were still considered a young team. We were starting to get good, and we had the attitude, *Okay, we're here now and you're not going to walk on us.* They wanted to show they were the better team.

I took a dirty foul personally and let them know, getting in their faces. The game was at a tipping point where it looked like a fight was going to break out. Luis Scola and Pablo Prigioni were in the mix, not happy that we were about to beat them. All of the players were getting into it and pushing and talking trash. Sure enough, Coach Rautins was right in the middle of it. He almost came to blows with their coach. I think some punches were thrown but didn't land.

It was one of those turning points as a team where we all realized, after, *Okay, we all have each other's backs here.* I felt like that was an important point in our development as a young group.

There were always crazy things happening with the national team. When we went to Las Vegas for the Americas Championship after that, I was hit below the belt against Uruguay. I fought for a loose ball with Esteban Batista, and he grabbed me in the balls. I punched him in the face and got a technical. They showed the replay on the screen, and the whole place started laughing. I showed the ref and asked him what he wanted me to do in that situation. That nearly led to another brawl.

We were optimistic about the Americas Championship. The US loaded up their roster for the first time in a long time, because they were hosting and because they wanted to get ready for the 2008 Olympics. That helped get a lot more attention for the tournament. It felt like a big deal, like we all got to be showcased a little bit, and at that time I still had NBA hopes. We went 4-4, which was good enough for fifth place.

Finishing fifth got us into the Olympics Qualifying Tournament in 2008. That was a twelve-team tournament in Greece that determined the last three berths for the Olympics after that summer. We went 1-1 and failed to qualify, so we went to Las Vegas for an exhibition game to help the US get ready for the Olympics.

That game was one of the coolest moments I've had as a player.

That US roster was loaded. It was the closest thing to the Dream Team since the Dream Team. They called them the Redeem Team—to make up for losing in 2004.

We had played them the summer before and I'd played poorly, partially because I was star-struck. As a pro, I wasn't supposed to get star-struck, but I was looking across at LeBron James and Kobe Bryant and Chris Bosh and a team full of guys at that level. It was such a good team that I was a bit intimidated, and I was worried about getting noticed.

Kobe would guard the best player on the opposing team, and he was usually a big trash-talker. That first summer we played, he face-guarded me everywhere I went. He had a hold of my elbow and would get in my ear, making train noises. If I was jogging, he was holding me and saying, "Ch-ch-choo, ch-ch-choo." If I was running, he'd pick up the pace. "Ch-choo, ch-choo, choochoochoo." I was thinking, *This dude just isn't going to shut up.*

I was a lot more comfortable the second time around. I had a little bit more swagger and was a little cockier. I told Kobe, "Every time I score, you've got to send me a pair of shoes."

Kobe was pretty quiet. When a guy like that is quiet, that almost takes you off your game more. At one point I crossed him up on the side of the floor. I crossed him to the left and took a step-back, and the crowd reacted to it.

So did Kobe. It woke him up. The next time I had the ball, he ripped it from me at half-court and took off for a dunk. The way he timed it, it was like he had let me catch up so I thought I had him, then scored. I tried to trap him at half-court after that, and he stepped through it and banked in a deep three. I thought, *What have I done now?* It was nuts how he could just turn it on like that.

There was another play where I got caught in a three-on-one off of a turnover. LeBron, Kobe, and Dwyane Wade were coming down on me. I had to pick my poison. I stayed in the middle so I could jump to either side. Well, Kobe passed to Wade and I slid over there, then Wade immediately threw a lob for LeBron. I turned over my shoulder, and LeBron was above my head. I looked in *Sports Illustrated* the next week, and there was LeBron dunking over someone with "English" on the back of the jersey.

I played well for the most part. We got blown out, but I had eleven points, which was second on the team. Moments like that made the whole NBA chase worse in a way. It was a lot of fun, but part of me was thinking, *If I can play like that and hold my own on offence against Kobe Bryant, why can't I go and sit at the end of Kobe's bench?* I was still at the point in my career where a lot of my focus was on the NBA, and I was always hoping to use those experiences as a springboard.

* * * * *

If playing against the Redeem Team wasn't the height of my time with Canada Basketball, the following summer was. We went to the 2009 FIBA Americas Championship in Puerto Rico and placed fourth, which qualified us for the 2010 World Championship.

That was our biggest accomplishment during my time with the program. Canada had been there with Steve Nash in 2002, the year I missed to help fish back home, and it felt like taking Canada back to the World Championship was a major step for us as a program. It was such a tough road back because the Americas zone was so good at that time and we never hosted anything ourselves, so we were always in a foreign country with foreign referees and no margin for error.

Things started out tough in Puerto Rico. We went 2-2 in our group stage, which was enough to move on but not enough to be comfortable. We started the next round with losses to Argentina and Brazil, putting our backs against the wall. We were 2-4 and had no chance to advance without two more wins. We blew Panama out, setting up a final game with the Dominican Republic where the winner would move on to the next round and qualify for the World Cup.

That Dominican team was loaded. Al Horford was playing for them that summer with Charlie Villanueva and Francisco García, who had NBA experience, and Luis Flores. They'd nearly upset Argentina in the first round, too. That game went right down to the wire. Every possession was so crucial, and every huddle was so intense. Jermaine Anderson had a monster game for us with twenty-one points, I had thirteen, Joel Anthony and Levon Kendall were good inside, and we managed to pull it out, 80-76.

I missed the final two games of that tournament to head back to Spain. Once we had qualified for the World Championship, the mission was accomplished. Baskonia pressured me to get back for training camp. The whole time I played in the Americas Championship, I watched video of my Spanish team trying to learn all the plays for when I got back. They'd fought me hard about playing, but I wouldn't budge.

I didn't get to play in the World Championship for which I'd helped us qualify. That was the summer after I'd suffered two cracked ribs. My season with Baskonia ended in late June, Canada was starting up in early July, and there wasn't enough time for me to recover in between. That was tough for me, because it was such a great accomplishment and I didn't get to be there.

It was even harder to watch, because we went 0-5 and finished twenty-second out of twenty-four teams. It felt like a lot of the momentum we'd built and a lot of what we'd fought to achieve had taken a step back. That pattern is still happening today, where the program makes progress and then loses it, a disappointment after every accomplishment.

There wasn't a lot of continuity at the time, either, other than with a few of us veterans. That was always the hardest part in a country where basketball wasn't as rooted in the culture as some of the other countries like Lithuania or as much as hockey was in Canada. The best countries spent a lot of time together, and that's always been difficult for Canada.

I missed the 2011 Americas Championship because of my wrist and ankle surgeries, and we didn't qualify for the Olympics Qualifying Tournament. When I rejoined the team in 2012, Coach Triano was back as head coach, and we spent the summer doing some training and exhibition games. It was mostly a summer to reset and try to re-establish where we were going as a program and get everyone familiar with each other.

Our focus became the start of the next Olympics cycle, where we'd have a lot of our young talent ready and a handful of veterans like me still in our prime. The year 2013 was going to be our new starting point. If I could get healthy.

15

BASKETBALL VAGABOND. OVERSEAS IV.

OUR TEAM CANADA ROSTER FOR the 2013 FIBA Americas Championship was the best it had looked on paper since Steve Nash was on the team. It felt like we were ready to turn the corner again.

Cory Joseph, Andrew Nicholson, Tristan Thompson, and Brady Heslip were all ready. The team had quality veteran bigs in Joel Anthony and Levon Kendall. And there were Jermaine Anderson, Andy Rautins, and me as the vets at the guard spots, with Andy and me providing shooting. There was solid depth, and everyone was excited about Jay Triano being back as coach.

In the lead-up to camp, I'd done everything I could to get healthy. I'd worked with Alex McKechnie to try to get my back and legs fixed, and I pushed hard. I was also still rehabbing the shoulder tear. My country needed me, and we had the chance to do something big. That was what was most important to me and what drove me in rehab.

I made it to camp with Canada ahead of the schedule I'd been given and started to feel comfortable. We had a longer camp, so they let me ramp things up slowly with an eye toward the tournament at the end of August.

I fell and banged my elbow in a practice early on. I didn't think

Carl English playing for Team Canada against Tiago Splitter of Brazil. The following year, Carl and Tiago were teammates in Vitoria, Spain.

much of it because it was the kind of thing that happened all the time over the course of a season. It swelled up, so we did some treatment and put a compression sleeve on it. Those things never stopped me from practising. It would swell up, I'd compress it, and I'd move on. Maybe we'd drain the bursa sac if we had to. I played through it and continued to do more and more in practice.

We went to Orlando for the next phase of camp, and by that time I was doing full contact. In one of the first sessions, I went to make a pass, and Aaron Doornekamp came to defend it. We met in the air, and it was an awkward collision where I was pushing hard one way to get the pass off, and he was pushing the other way. He blocked the ball and sent it back into my arm.

I felt something pop in my right arm, then fell on it.

The initial plan was to keep treating it like we had been. We'd always had an excellent training staff with Team Canada. Jason Meehan and Sam Gibbs were two of the best at what they did, and I had complete faith in them. Jason's a fellow Newfoundlander, so we became close. Even outside of Team Canada, I'd always consulted with them when I had injuries overseas and worked with them on my recovery routines. I would Skype or FaceTime with Jason to figure out a problem and how to deal with it.

As far as we could tell, this time it was still just bursa sac inflammation.

After four or five days of treatment, I thought something else might be going on. My arm felt different than other times I'd banged my elbow. The kickback wasn't coming at all, and I was having trouble practising. Usually this kind of thing was no problem to play through—I just managed the pain and swelling. This time I couldn't.

I left the team to see a specialist. That was a difficult decision, because it likely meant that I wasn't going to play for Canada in that tournament. I didn't want to go and take somebody else's spot and leave the team down a player if I couldn't get healthy in time, so we decided I'd fly home and get it looked at.

An MRI didn't show anything because of all of the blood and swelling from the bursa. The doctors decided that they would open up my elbow and relieve the bursitis that way. That procedure wasn't invasive and came with a recovery time of about two weeks.

When Dr. Amr Elmaraghy examined my elbow, he discovered that I had torn my triceps.

A triceps tear explained why it was taking so long to heal and why it didn't feel like other times I'd had bursitis. It hadn't been clear on the MRI because there was so much swelling in my arm.

It also called for a six-to-eight-month recovery instead of two weeks.

When I woke up from surgery, Dr. Elmaraghy had to break the news to me. He explained what he saw and what he had to do. Once he was in there, he had an obligation to repair the triceps. It would have been negligent for him not to treat the injury.

When he told me, I lost it. I was so upset, they had to put me back to sleep. When I woke up the second time, there were four doctors in the room, ready to keep me calm.

They said, "Carl, this is major," and I broke down. *Here we go again.*

* * * * *

This was supposed to be the summer I landed a multi-year mega-deal that solidified my family's future forever, then I'd pick and choose for a few years and retire. Instead, I had another major injury, and I was going to lose most of my season.

I had injured my shoulder, my back, my leg, and my triceps all in the span of six months, all right before I would have signed the biggest contract of my life. The entire time, my agent and I were sitting on offers. Barcelona was still after me, Darüşşafaka in Turkey had made a two-year offer, and a few other Turkish teams tried to keep me from them. I had over forty offers, and now they'd all be gone.

Teams started to wonder what was going on because I hadn't signed anywhere and we'd kept the injuries quiet. We kept pushing them off and figured we could resolve it after the Americas tournament. It was going to be impossible to keep it quiet now that I wouldn't be playing until later in the season. Injuries killed a player's stock overseas, because the contracts were so short for imports and everything was about what someone could do right that moment.

If I played at all in 2013–14, it was going to be so that I could show teams I could still contribute. I was right back at the start. And we didn't know how I was going to recover, either. My body had always been pretty good for quick recovery, but this was a whole new injury, and it was a long path back.

One small shred of a silver lining with the triceps tear was that I was insured.

The national team insured us for camps and tournaments. Every year, I went in and got a full medical, was cleared for practice, and then didn't have to worry about my contract or getting hurt and messing up my financial situation. Getting hurt still carried a cost in time and games and future contracts, but the direct financial impact of an injury was minimized through insurance.

I'd gotten injured in camp with Canada, and I was insured for half a million dollars. At least I'd be covered for the time I lost recovering and rehabbing. I wouldn't have to think about money—I could just focus on getting better.

I thought so, at least.

* * * * *

I did everything I could to get back on the court without losing an entire season. I followed the protocol, wore this clunky brace on my arm, watched my diet closely, and performed whatever workouts they allowed me to do.

The entire situation took a huge psychological toll. I was worried about my career. I'd only had ankle injuries before, other than the one wrist injury, and now I was dealing with the trifecta of shoulder, back, and triceps in a six-month span. It was one thing to get knocked down and get kicked. I had just been knocked down, kicked, and run over.

I spent a lot of the rehab process wondering, *Is this it? Is it over? Am I retiring?* I was only thirty-two, but I wondered if my body was giving out on me. I tried to tell myself, *No, this is not it, it's too early.* I tried to remind myself of the season I had just had and that I'd been in this spot before, starting over again, and had managed to make it all the way back.

Eventually, my attitude shifted. It became, *Hell no, let's dig in.* I was financially secure, I had two beautiful kids and would be spending a lot of my rehab time in Newfoundland, and I had people I trusted in Toronto who I was working with, making trips back and forth. I was going to fight through this like I'd fought through everything else.

I was still under the impression that I was insured. I'd signed my policy and left the paperwork to Canada Basketball, so I approached rehab as if I were covered. I made five trips to Toronto out of my own pocket. I was carded as a national athlete, which covered a portion of the rehab, but all together I accumulated about $50,000 in costs, thinking I'd recoup that money from the insurance payout.

Answers were hard to come by. I put pressure on Canada Basketball and tried my best to be patient. They kept telling me it would get sorted out. I talked to FIBA and the insurance company for clarification, and they sent me to talk to other people. I knew that insurance companies would want to find a reason not to pay out a policy, but I thought it was pretty clear: I passed my medicals, signed my insurance, and then got hurt, so I should be covered.

It started to upset me. It seemed like nobody had my back. I'd played for Canada for over a decade, sacrificed my body, been a captain, and given up off-seasons to represent my country. I hadn't done any of that for money or glory, but for my country. I'd helped rebuild the program.

While playing for the national team, we were supposed to have the security of knowing our contracts were guaranteed if we got injured. They took all of that away when they didn't cover the insurance policy. Now I needed them to represent me and fight for me, a player who had sacrificed a lot for them, and they weren't doing it. It hurt. It made a difficult rehab experience even tougher.

By the time I was healthy enough to play, I figured I wasn't going to see the money unless I fought for myself. I'm still fighting that battle.

* * * * *

It was a hard road back. Three injuries in such a short time had set me back to square one in my training. My legs were still getting their strength back after the back injury, and I was still getting comfortable shooting again after the wrist, shoulder, and triceps injuries, so I wasn't sure what to expect when I got back on the court.

Neither were teams. I'd gone from dozens of offers as a premier scorer to being untouchable because of injuries. I'd changed agents, too, because Justin Zanik had taken a front-office job. I moved to his counterpart, Andrew Vye. Andrew and I tried to keep the injury quiet. If teams offered good money, we'd come up with some reason not to sign. With some teams, I could say I wouldn't move my family there. With others, it was too obvious we were turning them down because I was hurt. By the time I was healthy enough to play, most of the offers were off the table.

I signed with Tenerife late in the season to show that I was healthy and could play.

I'd gotten used to spending more time at home during my rehab, and it was hard to be away when I went back to Spain. Mandy was pregnant again, and it wasn't worth packing up the family and moving there for six weeks, so I went alone. My preference was to have my family with me on the road. Ryder was about to turn six, Kirsten was about to turn five, and we didn't want to pull them out of school. It would have been too selfish to uproot them for a short trip.

Tenerife was struggling. They had lost ten games in a row and wanted to bring in a veteran to take some of the pressure off. The coach was honest about the fact that, because I was only there short-term, they might prioritize giving other guys playing time. The idea for me was just to let other teams know I was ready for next year, so that was fine with me.

It was late March by the time I got on the floor. It felt like a lifetime, but it still beat the timeline they gave me. I got into ten games down the stretch. My body had responded as well as I could have hoped, and I'd stayed healthy.

* * * * *

I went on an exhibition tour with Canada through Italy and Spain in July of that summer, 2014. Mandy was due in August.

That trip was stressful with her so late in the pregnancy. It caught up to me. It took a bigger toll on me than it did on her, which is all you need to know about me and my wife. I made it back from the exhibition tour in plenty of time, but I was still nervous about the pregnancy for some reason.

When Mandy went into the hospital, the room was extremely hot. It really stressed me out. Mandy was fine, but the heat was getting to me. We went in and the room was blistering hot, it was August, and she was about to have the baby. Mandy looked at me and asked, "Are you okay?" She said I was white as a ghost. I said, "I feel like I'm going to pass out," and asked the nurses to open the windows. They couldn't open the windows in a hospital room. It got so bad that I had to lie down on the floor. Nurses came in and took a look at me while my wife was calmly having a baby in the same room.

Once Kylie was born, I calmed right down.

Each time one of my kids was born, I felt myself change. I don't know what it was about Kylie, but when she arrived, I felt myself turning soft. She was the baby, and I'd let her get away with anything. All of the nervousness and anxiety washed away.

Kylie was also the first of my kids to be born in Newfoundland, which was special. Ryder and Kirsten were both born in Spain, and it's cool that they have Spanish passports and got to experience that. I was glad one of my kids was born at home—even if it almost made me pass out.

* * * * *

The plan with Tenerife had worked. I had established a market for myself again, even if it wasn't to the level I'd had before the injuries. I had options.

There were only certain places I was willing to go. I had always studied the international market and kept a mental list of places I'd like to play. The idea of returning to Spain was nice because Ryder and Kirsten grew up there, but I'd also done seven years in Spain and sometimes taken less money for the familiarity, and Kylie was a new-born, so the family wouldn't be coming, at least not at first.

Greece was somewhere I'd considered because of the culture and the beauty. AEK Athens were a former powerhouse that had just been promoted back to the first division after three years of relegation. They had a bit of a bad reputation regarding timely payments, but now they were under new ownership. They looked at me as a big enough name to signal to other import players that it was a safe place to sign, and I looked at them as an opportunity to play at a high level again and keep rebuilding my value.

We signed a two-month deal that had a buyout and an option at the end. That gave me some flexibility if the situation wasn't right or if my game took off again. It was a good fit, so I decided I'd stick around, and my family would come out and join me for the rest of the season.

The fan experience in Greece was as intense as anywhere. They were passionate about the sport and had songs and dances for their teams. It got so crazy that teams weren't allowed to have fans on the road. Every arena we went to was full of fans of the home team only, because the league was worried about fights and riots.

We had a road game just before Christmas, and our fans stormed the arena. The police had to come in with riot gear. They threw tear gas to get the fans out. It didn't matter that we were all in the gym, warming up. Our eyes were burning, and they had to take us outside for forty minutes to let the fans and the tear gas clear out. It may sound scary, but I loved the intensity. I just thought, *All right, let's go!* I scored thirty-three points in that game, and later, when we left, our fans were still outside, chanting and singing.

I went home to Newfoundland to visit for Christmas and had to be back for a game on December 28. I hopped right off the plane, went to the arena, and scored twenty-four points. The fans knew I had just made the decision to stay, so they went crazy during that game.

Another time, I did my usual thing on the road, trash-talking with the fans, when suddenly I saw something fly at me. Luckily, I ducked it. I looked, and it was a bottle of urine. A fan had peed in a drink bottle and thrown it at me! Our security came out and warned me that it was too dangerous to talk trash with these fans.

That season ended in the most frustrating way possible. We made the playoffs and were tied 1-1 with Aris in the first round with a lead late in the game. One of the guys on the team got the ball, and instead of running out the clock, he tried for a layup to extend the lead. He missed the layup, and Aris came back down and scored to win. Ownership were mad that we were out so early, because they'd signed me, made some other big additions, and changed the coach down the stretch. That was a lot of change all at once during the year, and it could hurt team chemistry.

I was irritated at the way it ended, though it was a positive season for me. I was back to being an elite scorer, finishing second in the league with 14.6 points per game and hitting forty-two per cent of my threes. Most importantly, I didn't miss a single game.

* * * * *

Canada hosted the Pan American Games in Toronto that summer, which would serve as a tune-up for the 2015 FIBA Americas Championship.

Going into camp was awkward. I still felt I was a big part of the team with other players and with Coach Triano, but the insurance issue still hadn't been resolved after two years and hung over everything. I put it aside to focus on the team. My thinking was, *I'm still part of this. I'm here in good faith.* They kept telling me they were working on it and that they were expecting a buyout number from the insurance company. I'd missed 280 days, so they had a number to work with now, and that should have gotten it moving. It didn't.

I played with Canada in the Pan Ams and thought I would go with them to Mexico City for the Americas. It was important to me to still be involved. I had a lot left to offer as a player, and I felt a deep connection to the program, to the young guys coming up, and to getting Canada back to the Olympics for 2016. That was still one of my biggest goals, and we had the roster to do it.

Sometime between the Pan Ams and the Americas, Canada Basketball decided they were done with me. People I trust told me they sat in on those meetings and were told they couldn't touch me because of insurance issues. I didn't understand. I'd put it behind me to come play, and they'd said the insurance was getting sorted out, so I started thinking, *What's going on here?*

Watching that team in the Americas tournament was gut-wrenching. Even though I was hurt by management's decision, I wanted more than anything for them to win and clinch an Olympics berth. I knew it would mean so much to the guys on the team and to basketball in Canada.

It came down to a semifinal against Venezuela, whom they'd beaten by twenty in the group stage. The winner would qualify for the Olympics. I would have bet everything I had on Canada winning that game, but they collapsed down the stretch and lost. It was one of the most heartbreaking losses we'd ever had as a program. I felt terrible for the guys, and worse that I wasn't there with them.

A lot of people reached out to me after, wondering why I wasn't there. It wasn't a "This team wins with Carl English" thing, but the team was light on experience and I knew I could have helped. The writing was on the wall at that point. I haven't been involved with the program since, not even when qualifiers were in my own backyard a few years later.

How that injury was handled and how my relationship with Canada Basketball fell apart were some of the most painful parts of my entire career.

* * * * *

Once I finished with Canada, I had to figure out what I was going to do next.

I wanted to jump back to EuroLeague, and I had loved everything about Greece, so we waited to see if Panathinaikos or Olympiacos were options. I was willing to take the risk of waiting if it was the right situation. Teams knew I didn't party, I didn't drink, and that I was a professional. They knew what they were getting, so if a roster situation broke the right way, they wouldn't hesitate to add me to the mix late, whereas some players might be a chemistry risk.

I was home in Newfoundland with my kids, training deep into

the off-season. If I had to wait it out, it was a lot easier to wait with them.

Not knowing when the call might come was difficult. I spent so much of that off-season trying to keep myself in peak game shape so that, if a deal materialized, I'd be ready to go in and perform from day one. I didn't like to use training camp to get into shape—I wanted to hit the ground running every time. For almost six weeks, my Greek agent said he'd have more information tomorrow, or later this week, or the next week. I was always ready to leave on a moment's notice.

The wait was getting exhausting and it seemed like a EuroLeague spot might not open up. We started to explore the other options available.

A team in Humacao, Puerto Rico, had been calling aggressively. The Puerto Rican league could be lucrative in the right situation, and they were coached by Flor Meléndez, who was a legendary coach in South America.

I signed with Humacao and put up good numbers. It was a fun experience. The country was great, and they housed me at a resort right by the beach. The style of basketball was intense and physical, which I enjoyed. And it was a shorter season, so I wasn't away from home too long.

The issue with going to Puerto Rico was that the perception of the league was not as strong. Teams wondered why I had gone there, and even though I played well, it hurt my market.

I tried something different the following season and went to do training camp with Bilbao in Spain in August. It wasn't a tryout the way NBA training camps were tryouts. I went there to see what the team was like and go through some exhibition games so they could see my game and determine whether I could still play at that level. At the end, we would see if there was a fit.

When the camp in Bilbao ended, Tenerife had an injury and reached out to me. They were now being coached by Txus Vidorreta, who I'd had my best season under with Estudiantes. It seemed like a perfect fit.

I signed a three-month contract and played well over eleven games. I didn't play huge minutes, but I was among the leading scorers in the Basketball Champions League, a lower-tier European competition. I averaged 15.2 points in 19.2 minutes and hit sixty-one per cent of my threes in those games, so I made the most of my opportunities.

Alba Berlin reached out when my Tenerife contract was nearing the end. There was a connection there, too, as their general manager was the same one who had brought me in to Gran Canaria and Estudiantes. The German league was strong and Berlin were a EuroCup team, so it would be another good chance to show I could still play at a high level. Tenerife allowed me out of the end of my deal to go to Berlin.

I went home to visit my family first. When I landed, I had thirty missed calls. The same player I had signed on to replace with Tenerife had been injured again, and they wanted to bring me back for the rest of the season. I'd already signed with Berlin, so I was torn. On one hand, it would have been nice to stay in Tenerife, where it was beautiful and I was comfortable. On the other, Berlin was a historic club, I hadn't played in Germany before, and I'd already given my word.

I opted to go to Berlin. It was tough to join a team in the middle of the year, because there was already an established rotation and hierarchy. My role was smaller, but I played it well.

Bouncing around was an interesting life experience, but it took a toll. I'd played seven straight years in Spain and then gone to Greece, Puerto Rico, Spain, and Germany all in a short span. I did the last few stops without my family because they were short-term deals and we didn't want to have to move the kids around so frequently.

Being alone made it a lot harder. I was in two places at once a lot of the time. Physically, I was in another country, and my mind was in Newfoundland. The first week I was gone, my kids called every day, all the time, and then it was a little less, and then it was, "Dad says hi." It was a lot on Mandy, too, having three kids on her own. We'd gotten used to the comfort of having each other close.

It was hard to play basketball in one place and focus on my family in another. That was life as a professional basketball player outside of the NBA. Maybe I didn't have to anymore.

16

Hometown Hero. St. John's Edge.

Basketball has never been huge in Newfoundland. It's a hockey province first, and it became a curling province for a while when Team Gushue won the Olympic gold medal. I was always an exception as a basketball player.

That was something I had hoped to change. I thought if I made the NBA, it would create a ripple effect where more kids would play basketball and the paths to do so would be easier. I knew having a strong professional and national team career was the best way to set an example, and when I was finished playing I would have a more hands-on impact back home.

While I was bouncing around the world, the sport was slowly growing in Newfoundland. The Harlem Globetrotters came to St. John's and sold out two nights in a row, and that opened some eyes about the potential interest in basketball. St. John's is a big and passionate city, and Newfoundlanders will always support their own if they're given the chance.

A group of investors started looking at St. John's as a potential location for a team in the Canadian NBL league. The league had existed for a while but struggled to keep teams in any one city for very long.

St. John's had a suitable arena with Mile One Centre and nothing to fill it at the time. The group that was interested included a few local business people with ties to the community and some bigger investors from away who thought they could make an NBL team work.

If I was on board.

One of the investors started reaching out to me while I was still in Berlin to see if I had any interest in playing at home. It sounded like a long shot when they first brought it up. It was a smaller-time league, and I had a lot of concerns about it. I asked questions and heard what they had to say.

I was also still negotiating with teams overseas. I always wanted to play for Olympiacos in Greece, and they were short on bodies for the start of their training camp because a few players were away for national team plays. I did the same thing with Olympiacos that I had done with Bilbao the year before: training with them for their pre-season. My hope was that I'd show them enough about me as a player and a person that they'd want me to stick around.

I fit in well there. They were getting ready to offer me a contract, and Mandy and I were already talking about bringing the family over there. I was going to be an insurance policy behind Vassilis Spanoulis. He needed days off during the season and didn't play as much in the Greek league as he had in EuroLeague, so I'd soak up his minutes when he sat. It was perfect, because at thirty-six years old, I was getting to the stage where I needed rest, too.

Kim Tillie, the team's power forward, blew out his knee, and that killed the deal. Using an import slot on a depth guard didn't make a lot of sense for them with a big hole at power forward. It wasn't going to work out, so I went back home to train.

I still had some overseas options and was trying to weigh the idea of moving my family again for something that wasn't as good an opportunity as Olympiacos. My kids were getting older and hadn't travelled with me the last two seasons, so our family had finally put roots down. I had missed birthdays and holidays and was getting tired of missing my kids all the time. To make them change schools and move again in grades two and three—it would have to be the right situation. My brother Kevin was also dealing with kidney failure and was set to undergo a transplant that winter. It was a crucial time for our family. The idea of being at home was very attractive.

I met with the group trying to bring the NBL team to St. John's, and we started negotiating. A second, more serious group came in and worked faster. They bought the team, called them the St. John's Edge, and immediately started negotiating to play at Mile One Centre. The Edge started practising at a facility in St. John's. It was funny, because I was training at the same facility just on the other side, so media would come down to do a piece on the Edge, and they'd pop over and interview me about them, even though I wasn't involved yet.

Selling me on the idea of playing at home wasn't hard, but selling me on playing in the NBL was. They wanted me to be a part of the organization from the top down. I'd be helping with front-office decisions, doing work in the community to build the brand, and I would be the face of the franchise. With an expansion team in a small league, it was hard to get the numbers right. I would be sacrificing a lot.

It took me two or three months to decide. I had all of the positives and negatives written down and talked to anybody who would listen to try to sort through it. There were a lot of negatives and what-ifs. My biggest worry was the quality of the play. My agent told me right off the bat,

"If you play in that league, I can no longer represent you." The basketball wasn't bad, but the league didn't have any credibility outside of Canada.

I thought a lot about what kind of impact I could have on the community and on basketball in Newfoundland. This would be different than the impact I'd had representing Newfoundland. People would be able to come to games and see me, touch me, and get to know me.

If I decided to play, I'd already lined up different charities and communities with whom we'd be working. I thought ahead to doing youth basketball camps and going into schools with the team. I would use the team's platform to inspire the growth of basketball in Newfoundland.

It can be hard for kids to find role models in Newfoundland. If I was playing at home, it would mean more for kids to hear that they could work hard and achieve their goals from someone who did it. I was an example of what was possible with hard work. I remembered what I had been through trying to get noticed and moving and trusting some of the wrong people, and if I was a part of the Newfoundland basketball community, I could help make sure the next talented kid who came along had an easier path and better advice.

Mandy talked me through a lot of the decision. She wanted to make sure that if I played for St. John's I enjoyed it. She knew how competitive I was and knew it was a risk from a basketball sense. She said, "You have to learn to really enjoy this. If you're gonna do this, enjoy it. There's not much time left, and it could be something you'll cherish for a long time." That's where I ended up. I thought, *Let's go at this with an open mind, take the league for what it's worth, and make this a really, really positive situation.*

There was a lot of good I could do, and I could start doing it while I was still playing. I could play with my kids after work and sleep in my own bed and drive in my own truck. I was going to be the face of the St. John's Edge.

* * * * *

There was a lot of buzz once I signed. I joined the team at a press conference on a Wednesday, and they'd only sold 600 tickets for the opener so far. By Friday, we were almost sold out for our first two games.

Everybody knew I was the best basketball player from Newfoundland, but nobody had ever really been able to see me. There wasn't as much social media when I was at my peak, and it was hard to find international games from Canada. I was almost like a myth. I'd disappeared, and people only ever heard of me. Now they could see me live, at home.

Our first game was in Prince Edward Island. Everything had happened so late that I'd only had two practices with the team. I was coming off of training camp with Olympiacos, so I still felt I was ready to go.

I was wrong. I was really rusty and struggled the whole game. But I finally found my stroke in the final minutes and hit a couple of big shots to make it a one-possession game. I was feeling the emotion and the rhythm.

There were thirteen seconds left, and Jeff Dunlap, the head coach, was drawing up a play. I cut him off. I said, "Nope, we're going to do this: I'm going to fake in, cut off of this here, come up top for three, and I'm going to hit that shot, and we'll win the game." Everyone stared at me. It was the first game, and I hadn't played that well. Everyone probably thought, *This guy is going to be a prima donna.* I told them to trust me.

My defender talked a lot of nonsense about being a defensive stopper, smacking his own chest. I looked at him and looked at the

Carl English of the St. John's Edge playing against the Island Storm.

referee, and I told them exactly what I was going to do. I told him the route I was going to take and everything.

I hit the three exactly as I said. We won 97-96, and we all walked right off the court.

The buzz kept building from there. We sold out both of our first home games. I was surprised how nervous I was. I'd played in bigger arenas and higher leagues, and there I was, as nervous as I'd ever been. It was one thing to play in front of 30,000 strangers. I was heading down to Mile One, which only held 6,200, but I probably knew 4,000 of those people.

It was also my team, which was extra pressure. When they did our introductions, they played me in to "Coming Home" by P. Diddy, and the arena went nuts. One of the guys on the other team leaned in and asked me, "Who are you . . . Kobe? What the heck is going on?"

I scored twenty-five points and we won, then I scored thirty-two in our second home game. The city was rocking. Those first games in St. John's were an emotional roller coaster.

I'd left home after grade eleven to chase a dream. To be able to come home and complete this circle by playing in front of family and friends was incredible. I was away for twenty years, ten months a year. I'd spent more time away than at home. I had this sense of accomplishment that I imagined the Spanish guys felt playing in Spain or the Greek guys felt playing in Greece. Instead of being a mercenary moving from city to city overseas, there was a sense of pride that this was my home and my team, and these were my fans.

Whatever way it worked out from there, I knew it was the right choice.

The year was a lot of fun. I tried to make the team as professional as I could while still having a good time. The guys looked to me as an example. I'd be the one policing the unwritten rules or fining guys for being late to the bus. They all followed my lead when it came to give back in the community, which was really important to me. Every day we were at home, we were at a school or a community centre or a hospital.

The team was more successful than the owners had anticipated. We averaged over 3,000 fans for the season, which was competitive with the biggest G League teams and was one of the highest marks in the league. We kept tweaking things from a business and marketing approach, trying to see what would work best to keep fans engaged. I tried to pull ideas from other stops I'd made, like players doing a lap to high-fiving fans after games or coming back out after we showered to sign autographs.

Every game, there were people who came up and told me they followed my career and thanked me for coming back. A lot of parents told me how much their kids were enjoying the basketball and getting into it, which was a big part of why I wanted to do it in the first place. All of the extra events and time could get a little overwhelming, but I'd hear something like that and it was motivation to keep going.

Being at home so often was great. Ryder was old enough to come out and help me stretch and warm up before games. He was also old enough to talk a bit of noise. He'd ask me after games, "Daddy, how'd you miss that shot?" I was finally able to share basketball with my kids regularly.

I didn't have any choice but to keep my energy up with three kids running around, no matter how tired I felt. It would get pretty exhausting, because the league had an odd schedule where we'd play five games in seven nights and then be off for a week, depending on arena availability and travel.

We had a back-to-back the first week in March. Normally, I'd try to nap on the second day of a back-to-back. The kids were super loud the whole day, and there was no chance I was getting a nap in. I said to Mandy, "There's no sense in me even going to the game tonight, I'm that tired."

I got into the game, and my legs felt heavy. I missed my first couple of shots, and then they started dropping. I hit three threes in the first quarter and began feeling it. I hit three more in the second quarter and had twenty-four points at the half. The rim felt like an ocean. Everything I put up was going in. I always worried halftime was going to cool me off in games like that, but I came out and hit four more threes.

I had forty-five points heading into the fourth quarter. Someone nudged me and said, "Hey, you're close to the record." I had no idea what the NBL scoring record was. It turned out it was fifty-six, so I was getting really close. If nobody had said anything, I might have gotten to seventy. The way I was playing, I couldn't miss.

Once it was in my head, I pushed too hard to get it. The other team also tried to stop me at that point, too. The referees didn't protect the players as well at that level, so on a lot of my shots, guys were closing out into my landing space. I twisted my ankles a couple times. I was also hunting. I took eleven shots in the fourth, which I'd normally never do. I tied the record with four minutes left and then missed a handful of shots trying to break it.

Eventually, I got to the free-throw line and broke it. I'd scored fifty-eight points on thirty-three shots and hit eleven threes. The Raptors' broadcast crew even mentioned it on the air. It was a really great night.

The season kept rolling from there. We made the conference finals, and I was named Most Valuable Player and Canadian of the Year for the NBL. It was special to be able to come home, do a lot of good in the community, play well individually, and have a successful first year as a franchise.

* * * * *

The second season with the Edge didn't go nearly as well.

I spent most of that summer resting, which was new for me and a tough adjustment. I'd tried to stay away from medication or painkillers throughout my career. If I took them, I kept it to small doses. Late in that first year with the Edge, I had enough aches and pains and my ankles were so bad that I was taking medication every day. I had always been a guy who played through injury if I could, and I felt an additional commitment to fans who were coming out to see me in Newfoundland.

Our season ended in late April, so I was going to have four months to get right. It was about recovering and running my camps for kids. I didn't do anything but upper body work and some leg work that didn't put pressure on my ankles. I only biked for exercise. I thought it would all help my ankles get better.

I flew to Toronto during training camp to get a bone marrow injection in my ankle. The doctors went in through my pelvis and took out bone marrow, spun it, and then injected it back into my ankles. It was amazing for a while. It was the first time in seven or eight years that I didn't have pain.

The issue was that the home opener was in a week. I was supposed to get the procedure done earlier in the summer, but the doctor was unavailable. They wanted me to take three or four weeks off. A week was really pushing it. We were sold out, and I was trying to do whatever I could to come back in time.

I made it back, but the damage to my ankles was done. It followed me around all year.

I'd always had a lengthy post-game recovery routine, but by then I had to take it to the next level. Before games, I was all about being calm and visualizing to keep me from getting nervous. After games, it was a different story. I would stretch, get treatment, flush out, work on my ankle mobility, do the cold tub, do hot-and-cold contrast, anything at all to help with recovery. When I was at home, I would wear NormaTec leg sleeves to help with circulation. When I was travelling, I had an FSM machine I'd bought from the Team Canada trainers that I attached to my ankles and back to run currents through my legs to help increase healing. The last four or five years of my career, it was probably a four-hour recovery routine after games so that I'd feel half-decent the next day.

A lot of things were wearing on me. I was carrying additional duties as interim general manager, the head of marketing, and the team's leader off the court. I knew I was the face of the franchise, but there was too much on my plate. We had a lot of roster turnover and made a coaching change. It was important to me that our players be role models for the kids who came out, and that wasn't always easy. Basketball became a lesser consideration after managing the team, travel, marketing, and community events. I couldn't think about actually playing basketball until I got the arena for each game.

My interactions with Canada Basketball were frustrating, too. They were playing a pair of FIBA World Cup qualifiers in St. John's in February, and I really wanted to be involved. We had done so well promoting the Edge, I thought I could help them out promoting the games. I thought it would be great for Canada Basketball and Newfoundland for me to be a part of it. I was ready to guarantee them a certain turnout if I helped promote it with them. But the insurance issue was still unsettled, so they wanted nothing to do with me. I tried to put it behind us and come up with ways we could both benefit and forget that whole issue, but they didn't want to.

It really hurt me. The rosters for those games were thin because NBA and EuroLeague players couldn't go in-season, and here I was still playing well and in the city where they were doing the games. I was a part of the program for fifteen years representing the province and the country, and I'd kept the insurance issue quiet, trying to maintain the relationship. They wouldn't meet me halfway or even part of the way. The games did poorly. It was a slap in the face for me and for the fans.

It was a frustrating year in every sense. I was still happy with the positive work we were doing off the court. Midway through the season, the Janeway Kids at the children's hospital designed shoes for me that I wore for two games and which we were able to auction off for the Janeway Children's Hospital Foundation. The feedback from fans and parents was always great. But for me as a player, it was a tough season. Overall, I was pretty unhappy.

Then I suffered a freak injury where someone tried to save a ball and threw it toward me, tearing ligaments in my thumb. My thumb was just hanging there. It looked awful.

That was supposed to end my season, but I came back a month early so that I could try to help win a championship. I was back for the second round and helped us beat Kitchener to get to the finals. I pulled a muscle in game three against Moncton and tried to play through it because we were so short-handed by then. The catch with taking painkillers so I could play through an injury was that I didn't realize if I was hurt until it was too late. I couldn't get my body right all year. We ended up getting swept in the finals.

For all of the drama of the season, making it to the finals was still a great accomplishment for the franchise. The Edge were becoming a big platform for me to make an impact around the province. That made the injury trouble a little easier to deal with. The fact that I could come home to my home province and make an impact, touch so many lives, and be a role model for kids to look up to was amazing. It was everything I'd hoped it would be when I signed on to do it.

17

CROSSROADS. PRESENT DAY.

I UNDERWENT ANOTHER ANKLE SURGERY during the course of writing this book.

It took about six weeks for me to decide if I would do it. The surgeon decided I should get an arthroscopic scope done to remove small fragments and shave down some bone to help with the constant pain I was in. Surgery is never an easy decision if you have a choice in the matter. There were times I chose to do it and times I chose to rehab or play through something instead. There's no way to know for sure what is right in the moment.

It's even tougher when you don't know what your future holds. I don't know if I'm done playing or if I have another year or two in me. I don't know whether, if I play, it will be with St. John's or somewhere overseas. I'm at the point in my career where I could be satisfied either way, continuing to play or walking away.

I opted for the surgery for my kids and for my quality of life. It had been tough to go outside and chase them around and be involved in their sports and activities the last year without a lot of pain and discomfort. If I was in that much pain, I had a problem.

Playing basketball for twenty years was going to catch up to me no matter what. Those are the sacrifices we make as professional ath-letes to chase our dreams. Whether I continue playing or retire, my ankle wasn't getting any better, and I wasn't willing to sacrifice playing with my kids pain-free. It's one sacrifice too far at this stage. I'm very active with my kids, and hopefully the surgery will allow me to play basketball, jump on the trampoline, chase them around, and do all of those things without hearing my ankle click and feeling it swell up and needing to ice it every day.

Any time I went in for surgery was scary. Every possible com-plication ran through my mind, even though I knew it was a normal procedure they do all the time. I've gone through enough of them now to know how lonely the rehab process can feel even when I have sup-port around me. Each time, it gets harder. I always tried to be mentally tough and keep things inside. This one was scarier because I wasn't worried about myself as much anymore. I have three kids now, and that changes everything. It changes when I fly, it changes my career choices, and it changes how I approach surgery in my head. I don't want to be a father who can't play with his kids.

Everything went well. The surgeon, Dr. Sagar J. Desai, said nor-mally this procedure takes fifteen to twenty minutes. He was work-ing on my ankle for over an hour. He couldn't believe the amount he cleaned up from my ankle. He also warned me that I have arthritis in there, and that means there are probably going to be difficult days ahead.

Despite all of that, I'm still here contemplating what's next.

* * * * *

My two years with the St. John's Edge felt like they had brought my life and my career full circle.

Newfoundland has always been such a big part of who I am as a person. It wasn't able to be as big a part of my career. I had to move away after grade eleven to get noticed for a scholarship. I had to go away to college to get noticed by the pros. I had to play far away from home to become the best player I could. I spent the first seventeen years of my life in Newfoundland and the next nineteen coming home for a few days or, if I was lucky that summer, a few weeks at a time.

From a young age I'd learned lessons about family and community and how people step up for one another. My early life was defined by the tragedy in my family. When my parents died when I was five and I went to live with Aunt Betty and Uncle Junior, I was lost and confused. They took me in as their own and supported me through everything. I always missed my parents, but I never felt like I didn't have people caring for me.

The support I always received was special. The whole town got behind anyone who needed it. When basketball became a serious goal, I had support from my aunt and uncle and brothers, I had support from Mandy and her family, and I had neighbours raising money on my behalf. Everyone did what they could to help.

I never lost that sense of home while I was away. There were times where I was too trusting or naive about people because, back home, everyone had always had my best interests at heart. I took that spirit everywhere I went and tried to make people feel the same way. My accent and some of our Newfie-isms would always get a laugh, but people also commented that the stereotypes about us being some of the kindest people are true.

Family and community were such large parts of my life growing up that it was always important to me to keep those connections. Mandy and I made it work for years while we were time zones apart. I only saw my aunt and brothers and cousins in the summers, but I'd sacrifice to help with the catch or take extra flights to get a quick visit home in between stops. Basketball came before almost everything, but whenever I had a choice in the matter, I chose family.

When Mandy and I started having kids, my life changed completely. So many of the lessons I had learned over the years came rushing back to the surface. There are books on parenting, but I learned so much about it from how people treated me. Everything became about my children. I was either moving them or missing them, and sometimes both.

My whole perspective on life and on basketball changed. I'm proud of a lot of what I accomplished, but being a father is number one, by far. A bad game is just a bad game when I come home to three kids who love me afterwards. Going through what I went through with my parents and then Uncle Junior, I know not to take anything for granted with family.

I think a lot of what I went through as a player dictates my parenting style, too. Mandy does more of the organizing, and I do more of the playing and goofing around, but when it's time to be serious, I can be strict. I lived my entire career with a strict regimen and believed hard work was the most important factor in success. My kids know that whatever they need to succeed will be there for them, but there is also accountability for mistakes. They know those mistakes don't mean we don't love them more than ever—we just want to teach them that personal responsibility. That can be a tough balance, because I worked so hard for so long to be able to give them things I didn't have.

This career isn't the easiest in which to raise kids, and I'm eternally lucky to have had such an incredible wife by my side. So much of what I accomplished wouldn't have been possible without Mandy, both as a mother and a partner. She was there with me through Uncle Junior's death, through going undrafted, through every injury and surgery, and through being a parent away from my kids. She's never wavered in her support of my career or her love for me.

No matter what was going on, I knew I had a person here who knew me when I was nobody, had the same values as me, is a terrific mother, and loved me. That kind of support allowed me to do great things. I respect her so much. She put her own career on hold for me when she didn't have to. She's smart and motivated, and I'm excited to do whatever I can to help her career along as mine winds down.

I have so much joy in my family, my kids, my wife, my brothers, and I have so much joy still when I play basketball. So much of my adult life involved being away from home and missing my family to have a career. The chance to spend two years doing it all at the same time was incredible. Basketball and the rest of my life no longer had to be separate.

As I'm telling the story, it seems like a pretty good ending. Then I pick up a basketball and I'm still not sure.

Carl English of the St. John's Edge walking through the tunnel and toward the court at Mile One Centre, St. John's, Newfoundland.

Epilogue

WHATEVER HAPPENS NEXT IN MY CAREER, I'm not making the NBA.

From the time I broke out at Hawaii to the time I tore my triceps with Team Canada, it was always at least a consideration and at most an obsession for me. There were years when I was consumed by it, and everything I did was aimed at making the NBA. There were years when I tried to put it out of my mind, and once I was having success, the idea crept back in. Making the NBA or not doesn't define a career, but it was my dream.

One of the most difficult parts of writing this book was revisiting all of my failures over the years.

It's been draining. I have accomplished a lot of great things, things that seemed impossible when I was a kid—which is uplifting. But for me, because I set my goals and my standards so high, there's been so much failure, too. Not making the NBA was a huge part of that. All of the things I did wrong leading up to the draft and in my first few years were a part of that.

Others may not look at it as failure. I had one of the best careers of any Canadian player of my generation. I was a fixture on the national team and a captain for nearly a decade. I played in the best leagues in the world that weren't the NBA, and at times I dominated in them.

I left home at a young age to chase a dream that I had no idea if I was ever going to see become a reality. The odds were stacked high against me as a kid from a small town in Newfoundland. I had no business dreaming about the NBA while dribbling on homemade pavement or shooting on a homemade net sticking out off the side of the highway. Leaving the island was an unlikely goal, but I accomplished it.

I ran into issue after issue after that. There was the teacher's strike in Toronto, my ankle injury during my redshirt year, Uncle Junior's death, going undrafted, receiving bad advice, getting cut for luxury tax reasons, missing a call-up because someone else got hurt, missing out on a contract because of a trade, and a series of injuries later in my career. I was never a person who deflects blame. Not everything was in my control, but I take responsibility for those choices and those misses. That's why the failures weigh heavily on me.

Nobody likes to fail. Nobody likes to lose. Nobody likes to deal with death and tragedy and heartache. Nobody likes to get injured right before their biggest contract. I had a life full of ups and towns that shaped me into who I am. I was knocked down a lot in my life and my career, but I always got right back up and worked harder in response. That's what life is, right? You get knocked down, but you have to keep fighting. It makes you stronger at every turn. If I quit, somebody else has won, and then I would be letting myself down, and I would be letting the people who have supported me down.

So, no, it might not be failure. I had a great career. I spent two decades playing basketball, which is all I ever wanted to do when I was a kid. I lived all over the world in these fantastic places. I have an amazing family. I'm proud of the fact that I couldn't be kept down.

Life is about the journey, and I've had a special one. But I didn't make the NBA.

There is a painting in my living room of me and the basketball net I grew up shooting on.

When I look at it, it takes me right back to those moments outside of Aunt Betty and Uncle Junior's. I can feel myself outside on the road shooting in the dark. I remember how my eyes would adjust after shooting long enough. I remember how my hands would adjust after dribbling long enough in the cold. I remember adjusting my jumpshot to a smaller rim or a thicker rim or a broken rim.

Basketball still brings me joy and excitement. What I love about the game shifted over time, but it never wavered. For so long, it was about coping. Then it became an obsession about getting better and better. As I got further into my career, I loved hearing the crowd or that nervous feeling before a game. I loved battling with a defender and trying to outsmart him. I loved my teammates and the camaraderie.

The game teaches you lessons, if you're open to them. I loved how basketball always brought new obstacles for me to overcome, whether it was how to keep my net from blowing over or how to get a shot off at the rim against a seven-footer. I loved how the old adage, "Hard work beats talent if talent refuses to work," always held true. And even if I did work hard enough, I got knocked on my ass a ton, and I'd better get up quicker and keep believing in myself. The self-belief basketball taught me is undeniable. If you don't believe in yourself, nobody else will. Here I was, a kid from a town of seventy, believing I could work my way to the NBA.

I still love all of those things about basketball, and it always finds a way back into my hands. I would dribble home from the bus, dribble while doing homework in college, and dribble around the apartment anxiously as an adult. The other night I dribbled for forty minutes just because I hadn't had a ball in my hands for a few days and felt like a piece of me was missing,

I look at my face in that painting, and it stares back at me with a lot of pain in my eyes. Back on that road, basketball was my escape from everything. It was how I coped with the death of my parents and then with the death of Uncle Junior. I've carried those tragedies with me my entire life. No matter how much time passes or how old I get, they are a part of who I am. They're a part of my journey.

The painting is perfect. My eyes look sad because that hoop helped me fight through so much, and at the same time it reminds me of all the joy I was able to find through basketball.

TESTIMONIALS

JERMAINE ANDERSON—Team Canada
The first time I met Carl English was at his pre-draft party in Toronto. At the end of the night, after going undrafted, I remember him telling a friend or family member that he was going to prove them all wrong. I ended up playing with Carl for a number of years with the Canadian national team, and I watched him dominate the international basketball scene summer after summer. I vividly remember in a game against team USA, Carl decided to start trash-talking with Kobe Bryant, and he embraced the challenge of competing against one of the greatest players to play the game. He did not back down for a minute and tried to match him basket for basket. Even though we ended up losing, I knew that I could always count on him to fight and compete regardless of who was on the floor. Carl ended up having one of the best basketball careers in Canadian history, and in my opinion he proved them all wrong, as he said on draft night. It was an honour to play with him, but more importantly, he's an inspiration for what he's been able to accomplish through his trials and tribulations. True Canadian hero! Much love! — Rock

ENGIN ATSÜR—Alba Berlin
If you are about to face Carl English on the court, you better get your team ready for a long night on defence. One of the top offensive players Europe has ever seen. Young players need to watch his highlights to understand the mindset of a pure scorer who achieved on the highest level internationally. To me, personally, he is the best teammate, friend, and exemplary family man. I will never forget the

times we competed on the court and the haircuts I gave him in the locker room.

MARK BAYNE—Nike Basketball

From humble beginnings in Newfoundland to a professional basketball career spanning the globe, Carl's story is about pride and perseverance. A Canadian basketball pioneer, his story is uniquely Canadian and an inspiration to all.

RANSFORD BREMPONG—Team Canada and St. John's Edge

I would like to say I've had the pleasure of seeing Carl grow up on the basketball court as I was playing with him at the beginning of his basketball career and then again in the final years. We played together for the first time back in 2000 on the Junior National Team as nineteen-year-old young men. Then we also played together in 2017 in the inaugural season with the St. John's Edge as thirty-six and thirty-seven-year vets. The one thing that has always stuck out to me about Carl English is how determined and driven he's always been to reach his goals on the basketball court. Even as a youngster, I don't think I've met too many other players that believed in themselves and their abilities on the court as much as Carl did even back then. That self-believe and confidence I truly believe comes from hours upon hours of him working on his craft to become one of the greatest basketball players our country has ever produced. Carl is a pioneer of the game and a legend that all current and upcoming players should pay homage to.

KAMIL CHMIELEWSKI—St. Thomas Aquinas

Carl carried around a worn-out basketball everywhere he went. He named her Destiny. He believed that it was destiny that would help him play professionally; however, I disagreed. It was his sheer determination and focus that would pave his successful career.

We were teammates at St. Thomas Aquinas, and while most of us were looking forward to the weekend, Carl was looking forward to practising twice a day. He taught me what it meant to sacrifice, ball above all. He has been a close friend for the past twenty years, and I am grateful to have seen his adventure through the basketball world.

Aaron Doornekamp—Team Canada, ACB Valencia

In my eyes, what makes Carl's career so special is where he came from at the time he did. This was pre–social media, before travel teams and national player rankings. He had to personally call teams to give him an opportunity, and finally, when they said yes, he was always their best player. His determination and willingness to do anything to succeed is unmatched and is what led him to have such an incredible career. I personally think if Carl were to be graduating high school in this era, we are talking about which top NCAA school he is attending, followed by being a lottery pick in the NBA.

Nate Doornekamp—Team Canada

As a player, there was no team he couldn't rally, and there was no situation that was too big for him. He worked his butt off, and the next shot was always going in. He is proud to be from the Rock, and his Newfoundland spirit was infectious. You can't pick your family, but if you could . . . I would pick Carl every time.

Melvin Ejim—Team Canada, Malaga ACB

Carl English is one of the most exciting players to play with. On the court and off the court. He has this incredible ability to uplift everyone with his energy. Whether it's hitting a three and getting you off your seat or his contagious grin forcing you to laugh and smile right along with him. He's been a great player and even more so a better role model for many players whom have come after.

Jaime Fernández—Malaga ACB

Carl English is one of the biggest competitors with whom I've had the pleasure to play with. He was ready to work hard and give his best every single day and every single practice. The energy, passion, and dedication he's shown when we shared team has inspired me throughout my career.

JOSH FISHER—Estudiantes Madrid, ACB
Playing with Carl was a great experience. I was fortunate to have that experience two different times with two different teams in our European careers. His dedication and competitiveness was on a very high level, which would challenge you every day and make you a better player.

MAURIZIO GHERARDINI—Raptors Vice-President, Fenerbahçe President
I truly appreciated his passion for the game and his love for his country: he never backed out of any opportunity to play for his national team, even when it meant taking risks in his career.

I enjoyed his passion for basketball, his curiosity in life on and off the court: discussing and sharing impressions gave me a chance to know him better and appreciate him even more.

A very good basketball player and one of the best natural shooters I ever had to deal with: he was dedicated, passionate, and always trying to improve.

PHIL HANDY—Coach, LA Lakers
Carl English was a name I quickly learned after I left the University of Hawaii to start my pro basketball career. Carl was one of the best players to ever put on a UH uniform. Had the pleasure of coaching and working with him on the Canadian national team for a few years. Hands down a top professional on and off the court. This kid made himself into a player and made a great career for himself. They don't make many like Carl English.

BRADY HESLIP—Team Canada
Carl has been a mentor to me since my first day with the national team. Over the past ten years he's been an incredible leader and mentor to a number of younger players, always offering advice and guidance. He always brings out the best in people, and I know everyone who has played with him would feel the same. A true Canadian basketball legend.

PHIL MARTIN—Hawaii

Carl and I have known each other since high school. He's like a brother to me. I've never met anyone like him. I can say so many great things, but something that stands out most is the level of determination, passion, and work ethic he possesses. He's driven, unrelenting, and has been inspirational throughout my life. I'm very proud of what he's been able to accomplish.

MALCOLM MILLER—Toronto Raptors, Berlin

Carl English! Captain Canada! That's my buddy and Berlin shooting partner. What a great guy and great vet to have in my life in the young stages of my career. Not knowing what to expect with the ups and downs of playing overseas for the first time, Carl was a reliable source of wisdom on how to refine my game and grow in life. He's a huge part of my success and learning on and off the basketball court. Still likes to believe he beat me in our shooting competitions, but I'm pretty sure I'm up 1-0 when it counted!

ANDREW NICHOLSON—NBA, Team Canada

My first impression of you was a very good one, actually. I knew you were a veteran of the SMNT and could easily tell you knew a lot about the FIBA game based on your dialogue with the team. You were very welcoming, and your upbeat nature made it easy for rookies like myself to feel comfortable and accepted on the national team. Definitely a national team teammate that I won't forget.

BRAD OLSEN—Barcelona ACB

The guy didn't know what a bad shot was, couldn't guard a pole. He had one lucky game against me. Carl English was the best backup I ever had. Thanks for holding it down till I got back.

All jokes aside!

I'll never forget the year before we become teammates, he dropped about thirty points in twenty-two minutes on me. I was sick that game—flu—I never told him.

One of the best natural scorers I've played with in my career. He always wanted more, and that's why he had a great career. He was never satisfied.

Also, 'cause he never passed the ball. Ha ha!

<u>HIMAR PÉREZ</u>—General Manager of Alba Berlin
What can I say? You are the first player I signed in my career when I became GM, and also the player that I signed more times, in three different teams! I love your passion for the game. I've never known any other player with that much focus in the game.

<u>LEO RAUTINS</u>—Team Canada, Raptors Broadcaster
When I found out Carl English was going to come home and play for the St. John's Edge, I was beyond thrilled—for Carl, his young family, and all the kids in Newfoundland he would touch. I have been preaching for a long time that a domestic pro league is critical for the country of Canada, for the opportunities that would come to players and the development of the game because of it.

Carl has been travelling the world working his craft, and many of his own people have never seen him play. For a Canadian player, for Carl, to be able to come home, make a reasonable living, and play before his home crowd, with his own children and countless others there to witness his passion, talent, and drive—it's a dream come true and will leave so many with an impactful and lasting impression. We all need our hometown heroes!

I had the pleasure of coaching Carl on the Canadian national team. Carl was an extremely talented player with an infectious personality— he could walk in and take over a room with his smile, humour, and gift of gab. At the same time, Carl was a challenge—his own worst enemy at times, and he often tested my patience. But, as with many other young men I had the pleasure of coaching, I looked at Carl as one of my boys, and I took the time to find out as much as I could about him and what I could do to get the best out of him.

In that quest, I discovered the incredible pain, suffering, and loss Carl had endured that I could not imagine any little boy experiencing. I saw how Carl fell in love with the game of basketball, and how it became his escape, outlet, dream, confidence, identity, and happiness. His joy and love for the game were evident as soon as he stepped onto the court—as was his imagination when he was alone, with just the ball in his hands. You can't be a great player without imagination—it was how Carl, with a makeshift basket on a highway, with no net, high winds, and cold temperatures, battled the best in the game, and won!

As an impressionable young man driven to be an NBA player, Carl overcame incredible obstacles to earn a US scholarship, represent his country, and become a solid pro. If not for trusting people who either didn't have the know-how, or his best interest at heart, Carl could have—or more so, would have—been the first "Newfie" on an NBA roster.

Carl's drive to be great, overcoming incredible odds, processing his painful childhood, and being let down by those he entrusted, gave him an edge—an edge that took him to great heights, and one that he had to battle with internally, that often became a deterrent to Carl, his goals, and his aspirations. A difficult navigation, to say the least, and yet completely understandable.

Carl English's life is a story of the highest highs and the lowest lows. A love story with the game of basketball and a girl named Mandy—his childhood sweetheart. It is about a hurt and lonely boy who became a success in every respect—as a player, a man, a brother, a father, a husband, and maybe most importantly, a son and nephew—to his parents and uncle, who are beaming with pride and smiling down at Carl, knowing their little boy is better than okay, and because of that, so are the many children and people in this world that Carl has touched and will continue to inspire with his life and his story.

Rob Sacre—NBA, Team Canada
I think of a clown and goof, but a hell of a competitor and always improving on his game. Great family man.

Melvin Sanders—Gran Canaria, ACB
First impression: RELENTLESS COMPETITOR, one of the best pure scorers if not the best pure scorer I've ever played with. A memory: On the road against Sevilla, I think, or maybe Granada. Carl comes

out and drops thirty in the first fifteen minutes of the game. Then he came to the locker room at halftime and said, "I should have had forty."

Sitapha "Taff" Savané—ACB Gran Canaria

I still remember Carl's first game with us in Gran Canaria. Pre-season trophy against our rival island Tenerife. He destroyed them. And from that moment on, I knew that if as a group we maintained a top defensive level, this guy could get us the buckets we needed, no matter who we battled. And that's how it was for two years.

But on top of being one of the best scorers I played with, he was also a great teammate. Extremely confident but also humble. Always participating in the locker room jokes, whether he was the one pranking or the victim of them. No diva attitude. Him being like that as a star player set the tone for the rest. This allowed us to overachieve as a group during those seasons.

Predraeg "Savo" Savović—Hawaii

Carl English: Dedication, team, leader, brother, family, fight, perseverance, BASKETBALL. It was an honour to have an opportunity to live and play basketball with Carl. His energy, dedication, sacrifice, and passion for basketball was and still is the example of how one succeeds, not only in basketball but in life. Of all the stories I could tell about us playing together, there is one I choose, a story of friendship and love for the sport of basketball we shared for twenty years.

Peyton Siva, Jr.—NBA, Alba Berlin

One thing that comes up about Carl is that he always says, "Hey buddy." Ha ha. Nah. First time I met Carl was in Lithuania. Great guy who helped me learn a lot about the European game and system. Hell of a shooter who wouldn't let me forget how great he was by beating me in three-point contests after every practice. Biggest thing that I take away from Carl, however, is the great father figure he is to his children. His kids idolize him, and he cherishes them beyond limits. Think that says a lot about his character as a man.

Rok Stipčević—Zadar, Croatia

Carl English. Let's just say it like this. Real PROOF where hard work, dedication, and passion can bring you and that are no limits in life and basketball! Basketball-wise, Honestly, you are far away from the most athletic guy I have seen, but with belief and the right mindset you can achieve your goals, as you did. These two things are the most important things in life, and you have both of them 100%. I'm sure that whatever you do in your life, you will strive for greatness, because that's you!

Usually when non-European players come to practice, they do their job and go home, no extra work. I don't know why, but it's like that, Americans/Canadians coming to Europe and they are doing just what they have to do. You were the guy who was always coming with me an hour before practice like you were my age, but you were ten years older, to work on your shot or to play one-on-one, stretching after and doing everything to keep your body in perfect shape, taking care about your diet and at the same time taking care of your family. There are not many players or friends or people like you. I have learned a lot from you outside the court and inside the b-ball court. Regardless of your past and everything, you are a real man!

Jay Triano—NBA Coach

Carl's journey is so inspirational. From overcoming obstacles where many would quit, he found a way to climb the ladder to become one of Canada's best basketball players ever. His strong desire paved the way for him to take his talents all over the world whether representing Canada or playing professionally. It's unfortunate that he is probably known better overseas than he is in our own country. He is a Canadian basketball treasure.

Kyle Wiltjer—NBA, Team Canada

Carl is one of the best dudes I've been around. He's the type of guy, when he comes into the room, you know Carl has arrived. He is always full of energy, and every time I've played with him on the court, he always brings the best out of you. He brings a sense of confidence with his trash-talking, but don't mistake this for arrogance, because he always finds a way to get the best of his teammates and friends. Super cool to see him build such a strong family, what he's done for Canada, especially his hometown. Nothing but respect, Carl!

JESSE YOUNG—Team Canada

What can I say about Carl? He is the only guy I know who can make a four-hour delay on a tarmac in Argentina fun, and that's how Carl with his infectious personality was always able to brighten any situation. I was very fortunate to have played with and against Carl for as long as I did and get to witness his greatness first-hand. Carl is an inspiration to all and a Canadian legend, but best of all, a friend for life. Keep throwing seven different styles of smoke, my man.

Acknowledgements

I would like to personally thank my wife, Mandy, my kids Ryder, Kirsten, and Kylie, and my brothers Peter, Bradley, Kevin, and Michael.

Special thanks to Blake Murphy, Steve Nash, Gord Pike, Don Coady, Flanker Press, Paddy Daly, Mason Gulliver, and Leo Rautins.

And for their kind words, I would like to thank Jermaine Anderson, Engin Atsür, Mark Bayne, Ransford Brempong, Kamil Chmielewski, Aaron Doornekamp, Nate Doornekamp, Melvin Ejim, Jaime Fernández, Josh Fisher, Maurizio Gherardini, Phil Handy, Brady Heslip, Phil Martin, Malcolm Miller, Andrew Nicholson, Brad Olsen, Himar Pérez, Rob Sacre, Melvin Sanders, Sitapha "Taff" Savané, Predraeg "Savo" Savović, Peyton Siva, Jr., Rok Stipčević, Jay Triano, Kyle Wiltjer, and Jesse Young.

GLOSSARY

360: The 360 windmill dunk was made famous by Vince Carter in the 2000 Slam Dunk Contest, and Paul George proved it to be repeatable in the six times that he performed it.

All-Star Game: The National Basketball Association All-Star Game is a basketball exhibition game hosted every February by the NBA and showcases twenty-four of the league's star players.

Assist: In basketball, an assist is attributed to a player who passes the ball to a teammate in a way that leads to a score by field goal, meaning that they were "assisting" in the basket. An assist can be scored for the passer even if the player who receives the pass makes a basket after dribbling the ball.

Backdoor: A backdoor play is when a player without the ball gets behind the defence and receives a pass for an easy score. This can be executed if the defenders are unaware of the open space behind them. Also, when a defender strongly commits on defence (e.g. tries to steal or deny a pass), they are vulnerable to a backdoor play.

Booster: Broadly speaking, a booster is someone who supports a school sports team. Of course, college athletics have all kinds of fans and supporters, including students who enjoy a fall weekend game, alumni who travel the country watching basketball, or community members who just like to see the home team win.

Coast to Coast: A slang term used in basketball to describe a player or team running a successful offensive play that starts at one end of the floor and finishes quickly on the other end, often quicker than the defence can react.

Combine: A basketball combine lets high school hoops players show off their athletic ability with timed/measured events like the lane agility drill, vertical jump, and full-court sprints. Unlike basketball camp, there's little or no basketball instruction involved.

Combo guard: A combo guard is a basketball player who combines the attributes of a point guard and shooting guard but does not necessarily fit the standard description of either position. Such guards are usually within the 6'2" and 6'4" height range.

Curl: The curl cut is executing a curl around a screen. This cut relies on the offensive player reading his defender. If the defence follows around the screen, then a curl cut is the best option to receive an open layup.

Draft: It is where teams in the National Basketball Association (NBA) choose players who have never played in the NBA before. If a team chooses a player, that player cannot sign a contract to play for any teams other than that team.

Draft and stash: NBA teams select overseas players, allow them to stay with their international teams, and then eventually bring them over to the NBA when the team and player agree that courtship is suitable.

Dribbling: In basketball, dribbling is the legal method of advancing the ball by oneself, as opposed to passing it to another player or shooting for the basket. It consists of bouncing the ball on the floor continuously with one hand while walking or running down the court.

Dunk: A slam dunk, also simply dunk, is a type of basketball shot that is performed when a player jumps in the air, controls the ball above the horizontal plane of the rim, and scores by putting the ball directly through the basket with one or both hands contacting the rim.

Euro step: The Euro step, two-step, or long lateral is a basketball move in which an offensive player picks up their dribble, takes a **step** in one direction, and then quickly takes a second step in another direction. It is intended to allow the offensive player to evade a defender and attack the basket.

Fadeaway: A fadeaway shot is a variation on a set jumpshot in which the shooter attempts his shot leaning backward, creating the effect of "fading away" from his defender. This makes it more difficult for the defender to contest the shot.

Floater: This is a shot used in basketball, mainly by the smaller guards who drive into the lane and put up a high arcing and soft shot in order to keep the taller defenders from blocking it.

Free-throw distance: The NBA, the NCAA and the National Federation of State High School Associations dictate that the free-throw line is fifteen feet horizontally from the plane of the front of the backboard. The free-throw line on international courts is 15.09 feet from the backboard.

Half-court: A dividing line that separates a court into equal halves.

Jumpshot: A shot with one or both hands in which a player leaps into the air and shoots the ball at the basket at the moment of reaching the highest point of the leap.

Layup: A two-point attempt made by leaping from the ground, releasing the ball with one hand up near the basket, and banking it off the backboard and into the basket.

Mid-major: Mid-major is a term used in American NCAA Division I college sports, especially men's basketball, to refer to athletic conferences that are not among the so-called "Power Five conferences."

NBA Slam Dunk Contest: Officially known and verified as the AT&T Slam Dunk for sponsorship reasons, this is an annual National Basketball Association competition held during the time of what is known as the NBA All-Star Weekend. The contest was inaugurated by the American Basketball Association (ABA) at its All-Star Game in 1976 in Denver, the same year the slam dunk was legalized in the NCAA.

NBA Summer League: Also known as the Las Vegas Summer League, this is an off-season competition organized by the National Basketball Association. NBA teams come together to try out different summer rosters instead of their regular season lineups, including rookie, sophomore, and G League affiliate players.

Off-season: The off-season is a period of time when an athlete is not participating competitively in their sport.

One-and-done: (slang) A basketball player who plays college basketball for a single year and then declares for the NBA draft.

Point guard: The point guard (PG), also called the one or point, is one of the five positions in a regulation basketball game. Point guards are expected to run the team's offence by controlling the ball and making sure that it gets to the right player at the right time.

Possession: A statistic in basketball defined as the time a team gains offensive possession of the ball until it scores, loses the ball, or commits a violation or foul. A possession in basketball is an important statistic because it allows teams to compute statistics on a per-possession basis.

Pump fake: A pump fake (also called a shot fake) is a feigned attempt at a jumpshot, restrained before the feet leave the ground. The pump fake is a fundamental move in basketball, used to cause defenders to jump or be shifted off-balance.

Rating percentage index (RPI): A quantity used to rank sports teams based upon a team's wins and losses and its strength of schedule.

Rebound: In basketball, a rebound, sometimes colloquially referred to as a board, is a statistic awarded to a player who retrieves the ball after a missed field goal or free throw. Rebounds are also given to a player who tips in a missed shot on his team's offensive end.

Redshirt: A redshirt freshman is distinguished from a true freshman; a student who is in their first year both academically and athletically.

Scout: NBA scouts are professionals hired by NBA franchises to evaluate player talent or opposing teams' preparation or strategies.

Scrimmage: A basketball scrimmage is a five-on-five basketball match that is often used to create chemistry between new teammates, practise plays, or evaluate skill in a game environment. A scrimmage normally occurs during practice with teammates, on a court during a pickup game, or against another team.

Seed: A seed is a competitor or team in a sport or other tournament who is given a preliminary ranking for the purposes of the draw. Players/ teams are "planted" into the bracket in a manner that is typically intended so that the best **do** not meet until later in the competition.

Shooting guard: The shooting guard (SG), also known as the two or off guard, is one of the five traditional positions in a regulation basketball game. A shooting guard's main objective is to score points for their team and steal the ball on defence.

Shot clock: A shot clock is used in basketball to quicken the pace of the game. The shot clock times a play and provides that a team on offence that does not promptly try to score points loses possession of the ball. For example, in the National Basketball Association (NBA), it may be called the "twenty-four-second clock."

Steal: In basketball, a steal occurs when a defensive player legally causes a turnover by his positive, aggressive action(s). This can be done by deflecting and controlling, or by catching the opponent's pass or dribble of an offensive player. Therefore, attempting to steal is a gamble.

Step-back jumpshot: The shooter takes a quick jab step away from the basket and takes a normal jumpshot. The move creates space for the shot, while providing more balance than the fadeaway.

Three-pointer: A three-point field goal (also three-pointer, three, or informally, trey) is a field goal in a basketball game made from beyond the three-point line, a designated arc surrounding the basket.

Tip-in: A score that is made by touching a ball into the basket as it bounces off the basket or board after a missed shot.

Travel: In basketball, travelling is a violation of the rules that occurs when a player holding the ball moves one or both of their feet illegally. When a player has taken more than two steps without the ball being dribbled, a travelling violation is called. A travel can also be called via carrying or an unestablished pivot foot.

Underclassman: A member of the freshman or sophomore class in a school or college.

Carl English grew up in Patrick's Cove, Newfoundland. He attended Fatima Academy and pursued a future in basketball at St. Thomas Aquinas in Toronto and at the University of Hawaii. Carl went on to achieve great success in the sport playing for Team Canada and for various European teams. Today he lives in Paradise, Newfoundland, with his wife, Mandy, and their three children.

Blake Murphy is a staff writer at the *Athletic* covering the Toronto Raptors and Canadian basketball. Raised in Cambridge, Ontario, he received a Bachelor of Commerce from Queen's University before studying journalism at the University of British Columbia. His work has appeared at *Vice*, ESPN, *Fangraphs*, *theScore*, and other publications. He lives in Toronto.

INDEX